Ignite

Your Purpose. . .
Your Passion. . .
Your Strengths. . .
Your Vision. . . .

ANNE ROSE

ISBN: 1482518678
ISBN-13: 9781482518672
Library of Congress Control Number: 2013902940

CreateSpace Independent Publishing Platform
North Charleston, South Carolina

DEDICATION

With humbleness and gratitude I dedicate this book to my family: my mom, Ingrid and my dad, Herb, and my boys Josh and Evan. Thank you for the ever so powerful life lessons. I love you more than you can ever imagine.

POEM ON LIFE

Today I choose to be me,
I choose to be free.
To feel good inside,
I'm no longer along for the ride.
I'm in the driver's seat,
And now I feel complete.
I now choose to believe in me,
For all to see.
The new me,
As I choose to be.

— Anne Rose

.

ACKNOWLEDGEMENTS

I am ever so grateful to everyone who has made this book possible. A book is written through the efforts of many. I am grateful to my parents who taught me that it's important to be authentic and guided me in the journey to find 'me'. They guided me and inspired me throughout. And the wonderful men in my life... you guys rock! Josh and Evan: you continually remind me to have fun. Every day I feel blessed for the incredible relationship we have.

Thank you to my wonderful editors Suzanne Simoni and Laura Pratt. Your hard work and dedication to this book have been incredible. And to my soul sister Jannie, I love you with all my heart. Thank you for your unconditional love, unending encouragement and belief in me and the passion I have for this book. And to my wonderful man, Bruce, I love you so much and am so grateful for the incredible love we have. And to Bryan Bennett whose words of wisdom inspired me enough for many lifetimes. You believed in me Bryan and always guided me in the right direction. My first coach, Samy Chong; you taught me the power of stillness, of inner knowing, of creating a path for myself; one that was so big that it scared me! This is one step in that vision. I am thankful for your wisdom Yoda.

Lastly, thank you to my clients and session participants. I learn from you every day. Thank you for your openness, honesty and sincere desire to create a 'better' life. It is an honour and pleasure to be part of your journey.

TABLE OF CONTENTS

INTRODUCTION

"Oh God, please, please..." she whispered to herself as she saw the inevitable. She looked in the rear view mirror and... Oh how life can change in an instant.

Just 3 minutes before that she was happily driving to a meeting, late one summer afternoon. She changed the radio station and began singing along to a song. Life felt good. She lowered the sun shade to shield her eyes from the bright setting sun before her. She was in her groove. A senior leader at a young age she was learning some powerful lessons about business. She felt she had it all: career, family, health and good friends.

In this moment she used all her strength to stop her car to avoid hitting the stopped car in front of her. As she looked in the rear view mirror she saw a white construction van careening toward her small sports car. 'Why isn't he stopping?' she asked out loud, as if the other driver would hear her. She grasped the steering wheel and held on, waiting what seemed an eternity before she heard the metal crushing sound of the van slamming into the back of her car.

This was the life changing moment for a young woman with so much life ahead. She sat, completely still for a few moments, trying to take in what had just happened. As she unglued her fingers from the steering wheel she began the inventory of her body. 'Am I okay?' she asked herself anxiously. Her eyes darted side to side as she perused in her mind every part of her body.

She felt no pain. 'That must be a good sign', she thought. She removed herself from the car and checked in with the drivers behind and in front of her. Both seemed to be fine. She had managed not to hit the car in front of her. She looked at the damage to her car. It was substantial. The back end of her car was gone; replaced now by the white van.

A tow truck arrived and dragged what was left of her car to a body shop for assessment. The self-assessment continued in the tow truck as she accompanied her car to the shop. Her first assessment created awareness that this 'I don't feel pain' thought was actually 'I'm numb and don't feel anything below my neck'. This was not good. The thoughts now flooded... 'How could I walk if I can't feel my body?', 'Will the feeling come back?' and 'I'm scared'.

This event was a 'boulder' event. We are often given nudges to remind us we are not on track. These nudges come gently at first in the form of a pebble. If that is ignored it is replaced by a stone, then a rock and finally a boulder. One way or another life gets our attention.

This boulder event served its purpose. It got her attention. This life changing event had the following impact:

Her priorities were re-set. Work was no longer the first priority.

With an injured body she began to listen to her body and give it what it needed.

She realized that she was off her path. This began a search to get back on her life path.

I should also tell you that this woman was me. I was hit on Highway 401 just west of Toronto. My path changed that day. I began the slow release of my corporate suit and began my joyous, fulfilling journey of finding 'me'. As I re-connected with me I began guiding others. I read books and took courses on self- improvement, self-analysis, psychology, authenticity and re-gaining my power.

I was inspired by Anthony Robbins, Stephen Covey, Oprah, Tom Crumb and more other people than I could ever list. Each step moved me forward. I struggled in moments. I wanted to give up the search and stay in my comfort zone but somehow a sign would appear and keep me moving in the right direction.

This book is to guide you along your path. Consider it a pebble. If you have picked up this book it's your pebble. Take the time, make the change, empower yourself, and give yourself the power to ignite your purpose, passion and strengths. Just envision it and begin.

With much love,

Anne

1   THE JOURNEY BEGINS

"What the mind of man can conceive and believe, it can achieve."
— **Napoleon Hill, author of *Think and Grow Rich.***

Barbara was in a job she dreaded doing. After hitting the snooze button several times every morning, her routine was always the same:

1. She dragged herself out of bed.

2. She showered in a feeble attempt to wake up and feel better about spending eight hours doing stuff she didn't like.

3. She mindlessly inhaled some breakfast and a HUGE coffee so she might feel more awake, alert and alive.

4. She hauled herself to the car and drove the same route to the office where she would chain herself to her desk for eight hours.

5. She tried to be a good manager. She strived to serve her customers well. She attempted to be creative in her work and problem-solving. But she didn't feel successful with any of this. She knew there was more. She knew she could be a more effective leader, could see her customers as the driving force in her company's success and get more enjoyment from her work. But she couldn't find the path to get her there.

6. She finished work, drove home and tried to enjoy the few hours she had with her family.

Barbara was totally unfulfilled. She stayed at her job because she was afraid to step out and try something new. Barbara was stuck. She was disengaged, uninspired, unempowered and lacking any vision.

Does this story sound even vaguely familiar? How about these statements:

- I want to create change, I really do. I've tried so many things and I still end up where I started.

- I've progressed a bit, but it wasn't sustainable.

- I really want to leave my job, but I don't know where to go.

- I want my relationships to be better, but I don't have the tools to improve them.

- I want more balance in my life.

As a professional life coach, I hear this kind of thing from clients I work with all the time; people who want to create positive change but need a path to follow for it to stick. Over the years, I've guided many to become more powerful, satisfied and self-achieving individuals. My work helps others gain clarity and examine their lives in a way that brings about sustainable change. I hope to inspire and empower you in the same way with this book, and I hope that my words teach you how to become your own coach.

This book will introduce you to a journey of exploration that leads to the rediscovery of the *real* you — the authentic part of you that knows what's right, that's acquainted with your true path, that's familiar with your purpose and passion, and that has the most potent of powers to help you to achieve all of this — and more. Allow yourself to ignite this within.

In this, the first of a four-book series, the focus is on envisioning. By creating a baseline of where you are now, you'll throw wide open the possibility of discovering where you want to be. Subsequent books will focus on empowering, inspiring and engaging.

Let's begin by exploring the true meaning of self-ownership, and how one manoeuvres most effectively through the streams of life. Via a series of self-exploration tools you will unearth:

- Your true self image

- The values that drive you

- Your strengths and knowledge on how to leverage them

- The key driving vision for your future

- The goals that will propel you to success.

Through the exercises in this book, you'll develop the tools necessary for bringing about the sustainable change you desire and uncovering a clear path toward it. They outline a series of progressive steps that will allow you to work toward the life you've dreamed of, one in which you're fully engaged and in a position to inspire both yourself and others.

Change Your Life

This is day one of your positive new life. On this day, you commit to a decision to take charge and make a change. On this day, you no longer allow others to make life decisions for you; you now own your own life, the decisions that shape it and the outcomes of those decisions.

Now ask yourself:

- Do I enjoy true ownership of my life?

- Do I listen to the advice of others and then make my own decisions?

- Do I follow my gut, or allow logic to prevail?

- Do I live my life in a way that reflects total ownership?

If you would like to change one or more areas in your life, find answers and adopt a new methodology for tackling your existence, you'll enjoy the process outlined in this book.

Together, we will look at your approach to:

- situations

- relationships

- people in your life

- tasks on which you're currently working

- responsibilities and decision-making

- creating a stronger, more fulfilled life.

Fear not: I will guide you down the path. Going through the exercises in this book will help you to find an inner strength that will allow you to conquer even the toughest situations life throws at you and allow you to re-ignite the passion for life, work, family, friends, your health and successes.

Today is the first step toward a better you. Declare your intention to travel it with self-statements such as:

- "Today I make a commitment to excellence in my life!"

- "Today I choose to leave the past behind and create a better today and tomorrow."

- "I will take it one day at a time, creating a better me day by day."

"Better" has different connotations for each of us. "Better," to me, means leaving behind things that don't work and replacing them with things that do work. This includes:

- your work situations

- people in your life

- your view of the people and situations in your life

- your home, car and work spaces.

What does "better" mean to you?

Getting to "better" may entail your making both minor and major shifts. You need to consider your options, and make choices that honour both you and your highest good. More about that later.

In order to create a better tomorrow, it's important to first be clear about today. Only with this truth can you embark on a journey along which you will authentically learn, grow and discover the real you. This is a trip, after all, and one that will take time, patience and enduring commitment. But, oh, what a journey!

Success Principles for this Book

As you start your own adventure, some practical tips to speed the trip:

Get a writing book. This can be a simple dollar-store notebook or a fancy pad from a specialty gift store — it's up to you. In this notebook you can do all the exercises from this book, and also use it as a journal to mark your passage of self-discovery. Call it *The Book of Me*.

The Action Chart at the end of each chapter is for creating an ongoing task list of your goals.

Allocate enough time to work through this book. You may want to schedule blocks in your planner every day or a few times a week to complete these exercises.

Go through this book in order. I suggest you not skip steps; each builds upon the last.

You can go through this book on your own or with a partner. If you choose to work with someone else, pick someone you really trust — you'll be sharing parts of yourself that you may not have seen in a while!

You can find more tools on my website www.innergizedsolutions.com. Let's get started!

2   THE FINE ART OF SELF-COACHING AND THE GREMLIN

"We choose our views, our thoughts and our intentions. When we take charge of those, we expand our view, allow our passions to shine and make the seemingly impossible possible."
— **Anne Rose**

Self-Coaching

In this chapter, we will explore the power of being authentic, and discuss strategies for capturing the gremlin that runs rampant through our minds and hinders our success. This part of the journey concerns itself with self-coaching. You will look within and discover things about yourself that you may not have been conscious of before, always with a view to unleashing your true self. You know yourself, sure, but you've likely learned to put aside your most authentic self-knowledge or given way too much credence to things you've heard about yourself from others that are simply not true. Whatever situation you come from, you are reading this with specific intent. There is no happenstance.

As a certified coach, I work with people who come to me for help with their work and personal lives, and we regularly conduct the exercises in this book together. If you're working with a certified coach yourself, you can make this book part of your process. You will find examples herein that are both personal and borrowed from my clients. Note that I have changed the names and some details of any client stories to which I refer to maintain the integrity and confidentiality of those relationships.

You may choose to go through this book on your own, completing each exercise solo and only periodically seeking input from the people who know you best. Or you may choose to go through it with a partner or small group. Your choice notwithstanding, I'd love to hear about your successes. You will find my contact information at the back of this book.

Throughout this book you will learn from the experiences and challenges of my clients, and also myself. If you're interested in my journey, skip ahead to "Anne's Story" and learn who I am, which of my stories you may relate to, how I overcame my struggles and where the whole crazy trip has led me.

What influences are impacting where you are on your journey?

What is Your Path?

We each create our own path. Our path is the direction of our life. It encompasses the choices we have made and the situations that face us on a daily basis. There are many influences littering your path. Among them:

- your education

- your upbringing

- the various roles you play in life

- your family institutions

- your current and past employment

- your health

- your economic situation.

Ask yourself the following:

- What path am I following now?

- What old patterns do I need to let go of?

- What path do I need to follow?

- How will I know if I'm on it?

It takes personal power to stay on your path. The dictionary defines power as:[i]

1. the ability to do or act; capability of doing or accomplishing something.

2. political or national strength: the balance of power in Europe.

3. great or marked ability to do or act; strength; might; force.

But this definition isn't a good indicator of the power we hold fiercely within us, because true power is power that comes from deep inside, way down deep in the pit of your stomach. It's the power we use as individuals to cultivate greatness in our lives. At the same time, it's a universal power; the power that some refer to as God, Allah, Buddha, the universe or "the collective." It's a belief that you have a path to follow, and a purpose in your life.

We are often presented with signs alerting us to the need to make a course correction, especially when we are misdirected on our path. If we ignore them, they amplify to get our attention. The signs first comes quietly, like a small pebble, and then it gets bigger, like a stone, then a rock, then a boulder. Each message gets progressively louder to get our attention until we create the change and actionize it to bring us back on our path.

Footprints on the sands of time are not made by sitting down.
— Unknown

I often use the analogy of having your feet stuck in cement to describe what it's like to be off the path and temporarily immobilized such that you can't take another step. You may have experienced this feeling. If you have, you know it's hard to move forward when your feet are glued in place. You may have even lost sight of the path. Clients remind me of this as we start to close in on the path and they tell me they can't remember what it was like to be "on track" as they've been "off" it for so long.

If this concept resonates and you feel a sense of being off your path, ask yourself:

1. Am I going forward or am I staying here?

2. Is the concrete that's currently locking down my feet powerful enough to stop the will within me and the desire to succeed, or might I allow my own personal power to break the blocks and freely float up above the broken concrete chunks?

As you achieve greater and greater freedom, the tiny stones that have collected at your feet from the concrete will be cleared away by the winds that caress you and take you to the next destination, the destination that delivers you one step closer to the greatness, challenge, self-worth and energy that are given to you, as they are to each of us, for meaningful improvement as individuals and human beings.

Now that you have an idea of how willing you really are to step into your power, let's consider what is possible. Answer the following:

1. What would it be like to fully step into your power?

2. How will you know you have achieved this?

3. What moves can you make to step even more fully into your power?

Hello, Gremlin!

So you've found your power! Great! Now let's work on keeping it. There's an inherent part of us that will resist any change, trying to take back that power. This is the same part that questions and challenges and creates resistance when we seek to introduce change or try something new. This part doubts the things we attempt. You are familiar with this internal voice. It's the one that fills your head with such pessimistic thoughts as:

- It will never work.

- I don't have enough time.

- I don't have the money.

- I don't have the necessary tools.

- I've tried this already and failed.

- It will be too hard.

- I am too fat, skinny, short or tall.

- Why am I bothering with this?

- I should give up now before I *really* fail.

This part of us is often referred to as our internal critic or as a gremlin as described by Rick Carson[1]. The gremlin derives from the ego part of our true self. The ego is the inauthentic part of us. It's learned but, as Eckhart Tolle explains[2] it's an essential component of our make-up. Worse, it believes we cannot be successful. The ego is hard-wired to resist our efforts to create a better self, a better life, a better job, etc.

Our true self is the authentic part of who we are. This is the part that is aware of our purpose, passions and overall life mission. It is equipped with the tools to achieve them, and knows that we are successful right in this moment. At any given point in the day, we have chosen what part of ourselves will guide our

> *He who would be useful, strong and happy must cease to be a passive receptacle for the negative, beggarly and impure streams of thought; and as a wise householder commands his servants and invites his guests, so must he learn to command his desires and to say, with authority, what thoughts he shall admit into the mansion of his soul.*
> — *James Allen*

---

1. Rick Carson, Taming Your Gremlin
2. Eckhart Tolle, *The Power of Now and A New Earth,*

actions and behaviours: our inauthentic self (i.e., our gremlin self) or our authentic self.

If, you make a choice to allow the authentic part of you to lead, you can guide the gremlin out of your head and into a place of neutrality or positivity.

Getting the Gremlin Out of Your Head

Here are some options for your gremlin:

1. When the gremlin pops up its head, acknowledge it by saying, "Hello, gremlin!" You may want to name your gremlin. It can be the name of someone you know, a character from a movie or TV show, someone in the public eye or just a name that seems to capture that negative, doubt-filled part of you. One of my clients, Joseph, named his gremlin Mervin.

2. Create a figurative place in your mind for your gremlin to go. When Joseph was looking for a place to send Mervin, he visualized a decorative cookie jar. Joseph guided his gremlin in there and pushed the top down but, within a moment, Mervin had popped that lid off and was back in full force. With the new understanding that he'd need a sturdier method of containment and a tighter-fitting lid, Joseph devised a safety deposit box that was strong enough to hold his gremlin. Best of all, only Joseph had the key! He put all sorts of things in that box that he thought Mervin would like, including a flat-screen TV, video games, yummy food and comfy furniture. It worked! So now when Mervin pops up, Joseph thanks him and send him to the safety deposit box. Go ahead and create whatever container you like for your own gremlin — just make sure it has a tight-fitting lid!

3. Send your gremlin off to do a task. Gremlins can help solve a problem that's been plaguing you. Clients have told me they've sent their gremlins to wash dishes, fold laundry and even deal with difficult bosses!

Know that as you embark and continue on this journey to rediscover yourself, your gremlin will likely pop up. Remember your choices when it does. I find that if the gremlin comes up strongly, it's often just before a good breakthrough. The gremlin will instinctively fight against creating positive change. Be aware of it and address it as such. Know that something really great is likely just around the corner!

The Gremlin Exercise

My gremlin's name is: _____

In the blank space below, draw a picture of your gremlin. If you prefer, cut a picture out of a newspaper or magazine that best depicts your gremlin.

Ready?

In the next chapter, you'll begin establishing a baseline. Here, you will find answers to the following questions:

- What are my key driving values?

- What makes me get up in the morning and say "yeah!"?

Remember, each exercise and chapter builds upon the last, so you'll deepen your understanding of who you are, what's important to you and how to achieve your best life as we go along.

Action Chart

Action	Date	Dependencies/Risks

3   UNEARTHING YOUR
NEEDS AND VALUES

*"Pure joy will follow and so will the day you
truly begin to live your purpose."*
— **Bill Cohen**

Needs and Values

In chapter 4, you will create a statement of your mission or purpose in life. To craft the statement, we'll begin by assessing your needs and values and then look at your strengths.

Values are essential to the understanding of who we are and why we react to stimuli, external and internal, the way we do. They drive our interactions, form the basis of our hot buttons and shape how we work with others. Uncovering and understanding your values allows you to know the authentic you, to set goals and to be clear about your path. It's foundational stuff, this, and that's why we start this chapter with identifying values. Upon these, all else is built.

> *"Life's ups and downs provide windows of opportunity to determine your values and goals. Think of using all obstacles as stepping stones."*
> — *Marsha Sinetar*

Values are predicated on needs. To really understand our values, we must take stock of our needs. Each of us has certain basic human requirements, regardless of who we are, where we live, our age, or whether we're male or female. Abraham Maslow identified these needs and presented them in a pyramid shape.

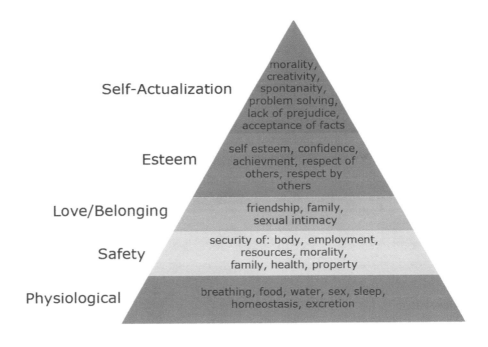

Self-Actualization — morality, creativity, spontanaity, problem solving, lack of prejudice, acceptance of facts

Esteem — self esteem, confidence, achievment, respect of others, respect by others

Love/Belonging — friendship, family, sexual intimacy

Safety — security of: body, employment, resources, morality, family, health, property

Physiological — breathing, food, water, sex, sleep, homeostasis, excretion

Each human hits this planet with a different set of requirements. Once these requirements are fulfilled, we experience a sense of peace and achievement. I believe that we invest most of our lives in pursuit of fulfilling the needs that are most important to us. We call these key values. We'll explore this further in the next section. In Maslow's pyramid, these are featured in the top four sections.

Let's look at each level in isolation. The first level of needs is physiological. In general terms, our physiological needs include food, shelter, water and breath.

Level two is the need to feel safe from the elements of nature and danger. Safety at work is a need, as is safety at home.

Level three is concerned with love and belonging. These socially oriented needs include our need to be with others and to feel a sense of family.

Level four deals with esteem. This is your need to feel respected by the people in your work and home life. It includes a need for feelings of accomplishment, fulfillment and satisfaction. An absence of any of these can challenge our self-confidence and ultimately hinder our business and career success.

The final level of Maslow's needs is self-actualization. This can be somewhat elusive in its truest meaning. The Merriam-Webster dictionary defines self-actualization as: "to realize fully one's potential." [ii]

Maslow identified eight ways to self-actualize. [iii] They serve as wonderful lessons for growth.

1. Experience things fully, vividly, selflessly. Throw yourself into the experiencing of something. Concentrate on it wholly. Let it absorb you totally.

2. Life is an ongoing process of choosing between safety (out of fear and need for defense) and risk (for the sake of progress and growth). It's about stepping out of your comfort zone every once in a while.

3. Let the self emerge. Try to shut out the external clues nudging you on what to think, feel, say and so on, and let your experience enable you to say what you truly feel.

4. When in doubt, be honest. If you look into yourself and are truthful, you will also take responsibility. Taking responsibility is self-actualizing.

5. Listen to your own tastes. Be prepared to be unpopular.

6. Use your intelligence, and work to do the things you want to do well — no matter how insignificant they might seem.

7. Make peak experiencing more likely; get rid of illusions and false notions. Learn what you are good at and what you're not so good at.

8. Find out who you are, what you are, what you like and don't like, what is good and what is bad for you, where you are going and what your mission is. Opening up to yourself in this way is a means of identifying defenses — and then finding the courage to give them up. That's what this book is about.

Wants, meanwhile, are those things we need neither to sustain life, nor to reach a point of personal fulfillment therein. They are merely things that we have identified as "nice-to-haves." The media have a lot to answer for in this department. Have you ever been watching TV, feeling quite content, only to see a commercial for a candy bar that you immediately *must* have? We don't *need* that candy bar to sustain life or enhance its fulfillment; but the power of suggestion has driven us to *want* one.

Awareness of all of these aspects of self provides insight into why one person may respond the way she does in certain situations, and another may respond quite differently. It also provides a reference point for growth. For each of the key areas listed below, identify the associated needs and evaluate your current level of satisfaction for each. Use a 1-10 scale, with one being low, five being average and 10 being high.

Physiological Needs

_____

_____

_____

_____

_____

_____

Safety Needs

_____

_____

_____

_____

_____

_____

_____

Love/Belonging Needs

_____

_____

_____

_____

_____

_____

Esteem Needs

_____

_____

_____

_____

_____

_____

Self-Actualization Needs

_____

_____

_____

_____

_____

_____

_____

Your Key Driving Values

At the root of our needs lie our personal values. A good definition of values is: "relative worth, merit or importance: *the value of a college education; the value of a queen in chess*."[iv] Values are the things that mean the most to us; they have worth. Our values often act as indicators of what is right and what is wrong in our lives.

Values are a function of a number of things, including:

- your family

- your cultural heritage

- traumatic situations you've experienced

- your education

- your friends

- your exposure to the media.

Our values are influenced by every interaction we have, every TV show and movie we watch, every book we read, every activity in which we engage. Still, our fundamental, core values don't change. You are who you are, after all. In essence, you are every moment of your life that you've experienced until this moment in time.

Imagine the possibilities here. If you know what values are most important to you, you can make better decisions, both for the short and long term. In a case example, we find Stacey at a crossroads. She has worked in the pharmaceutical industry for 17 years and, while she's enjoyed her job, that sense of satisfaction has been decreasing for the last five years. Stacey's children have just moved out to attend universities in different cities. She is feeling lonely and unfulfilled. She has always enjoyed music, but doesn't really know what to do with that sense of pleasure. She learned to play piano when she was seven, and has kept it up ever since. By exploring her values through a values exercise, she identified her top five values as: harmony, peace, adventure, balance and creativity. She looked at these and asked herself: "In which profession could I have all of these met while incorporating my love of music?" She talked to people who had some component of music in their jobs and looked carefully at different career choices. Based on the results of this and an acknowledgement of her values, Stacey chose to start teaching music part-time from her home. This balance fulfilled her and enhanced her feelings about her full-time employment. For Stacey, this part-time teaching gig was enough to honour her values.

At times, your core values may take a back seat to inauthenticity. It is then that external influences are so great that one's core values are shaken and other values are given room to take over. You may watch your stress levels shoot to the ceiling. You may feel frustrated, angry, irritated, unworthy and unmotivated. You may feel invaluable, insignificant or unimportant. You may experience the sense that you're being ignored, disregarded, challenged, put down or even ridiculed. It's a highly uncomfortable, unnatural state. Indeed, you may feel so uncomfortable with your behaviour that you question afterward why you ever went that way. We're granted the gift of clear signs when we're acting inauthentically. It's at this point that we have the choice to continue in that fashion or not.

Achieving a state of clarity on your values aids you in all areas of your life: work, relationships, family, career decisions, personal growth and quest for success. When we honour our values and others around us do, too, we feel motivated, happy and creative. The satisfaction of this state can inspire feelings of contentment, productivity and being totally in one's groove! Our problem-solving prowess increases in this place, too, as does our commitment to a task and our people skills.

In this chapter, you'll do a series of progressive, introspective exercises that will define your values, identify how and where you're living them, and offer guidance on creating positive changes that impact each area of your life.

So, let's get started! You will complete a series of values exercises, each getting you closer to a clear, personal definition and application of your values.

Values Clarification Exercise

Here's a simple exercise for identifying your top values. Don't move on from this until you've completed it.

1. Review the values list on the next two pages. Put a check mark next to any that resonate. Use this catalogue as a reference when devising your own values list. These are only suggestions; there's an infinite number of values that may appear on *your* list.

Abundance	Close relationships	Emotional health	Hope
Acceptance	Collaboration	Encouragement	Humility
Accomplishment	Commitment	Enjoyment	Humour
Accuracy	Communication	Equality	Inclusion
Achievement	Community	Excellence	Independence
Acknowledgement	Competition	Excitement	Influencing others
Advancement	Completion	Faith	Infusion
Adventure	Confidence	Family	Inspiration
Aesthetics	Connection	Flexibility	Integration
Affection	Connectedness	Flow	Integrity
Affiliation	Congruence	Focus	Inner harmony
Aloneness	Consciousness	Forgiveness	Inner peace
Appreciation	Contribution	Friendship	Intellectual status
Authenticity	Cooperation	Freedom	Intimacy
Autonomy	Courage	Free spirit	Intuition
Balance	Camaraderie	Fun	Job tranquility
Being	Country	Gentleness	Joy
Beauty	Creativity	Growth	Justice
Bliss	Delivery	Grace	Knowing
Bonding	Decisiveness	Harmony	Kindness
Calling	Discipline	Having a family	Kaizen
Cause	Directness	Health	Knowledge
Change and variety	Effectiveness	Helping other people	Lack of pretense
Challenging problems	Elegance	Helping society	Leadership
Chemistry	Empathy	Honesty	Learning
Clarity	Empowerment	Honour	Legacy
Lightness	Process	Selflessness	Values
Listening	Power	Sensitivity	Variety
Location	Profit	Sensuality	Vision
Love	Promise-keeping	Serenity	Vitality

Loyalty	Productivity	Service	Wealth
Magic	Public Service	Silence	Wholeness
Market position	Purity	Solitude	Win-Win
Mastery/ excellence	Purpose	Sophistication	Wisdom
Meaningful work	Quality relationships	Soul space	Wonder
Merit	Questions	Soul work	Work under pressure
Miracles	Recognition	Spontaneity	Working alone
Money	Relationship	Spirituality	Working with others
Motivation	Respect	Stability	Yin-Yang
Nature	Responsibility	Status	Zest
Nurturing	Result	Success	
Openness	Rewards	Supervising others	
Orderliness	Risk-taking	Teamwork	
Participation	Romance	Time freedom	
Partnership	Sacredness	To be known	
Peace	Safety	Tradition	
Performance	Sanctuary	Tranquility	
Personal goal	Security	Transformation	
Personal power	Self-esteem	Trust	
Play	Self-expression	Truth	
Privacy	Self-respect	Truthfulness	

2. Now that you've selected a first-pass choice of words, conduct a second pass to narrow your choices. Consider only the words with check marks. Compare each and put a second check mark next to any value that you feel has a particular significance.

3. Take out 10 to 30 sheets of small notepaper or Post-it notes — each piece should be big enough to contain just one or two words.

4. On each, write down one value from your values exercise. Don't stop until you've written as many values as you have. Lay all the bits of paper in front of you and take stock of the words you've written on them.

5. With each, ask yourself, "Would I crawl over broken glass to achieve this?" If your answer is yes, leave it in your active pile. If not, put that value aside. It doesn't mean it isn't important; it only means it's not *as* important as the others.

6. Put your values in order of importance. Remember that there are no right or wrong answers, no good or bad. You are simply identifying *your* highest-ranking values. Each one is important! Here's how to do it:

    i. Imagine you're just about to embark on a wonderful trip that you have planned for months, maybe even years. You have just flown to a beautiful sunny location where the *Empress Value* cruise ship is docked. As you approach the cruise ship, you are told that price of entry is one value. In order to board this wonderful floating city you must discard one of your values. Which one will you select? Turn it face down beside the remaining values.

    ii. Once you have released that value, you board and make your way to your cabin. As you unlock the door you realize that the room is not only incredibly small, but it's an inside cabin. You had expressly directed your travel agent to get you an outside cabin. You look at your confirmation and there is no mention of an outside cabin, only a room number. One of the Room Stewards comes by and you explain your situation. He kindly offers you an upgrade to an outside cabin. The cost: one value. Choose one value to discard. Place this value face down, on top of the first value you discarded.

iii. Once you've settled into your nice outside cabin it's time for dinner. In the dining room you are escorted to your table where you join the other 8 dining guests. After brief introductions two of your table mates begin to argue. In fairly short order it becomes uncomfortable for the rest of the guests. You mutter to yourself that you have to change tables. You approach the maitre'd and explain the situation. He offers to move you to another table with a group of people that you assess to be much more in line with the experience you were expecting. Of course, this comes with a cost. You guessed it... surrender one value and join the new table.

iv. After a delicious meal with wonderful company you decide to take a stroll on the main deck. It's a beautiful night and the stars are shining brightly. You hear some really good music coming from further up on that deck. You approach the door and know you just have to get in to marinade in the music. You try your room key to get in but it's denied. The Cruise Director comes out and informs you that it is a private party for invited guests only. You really want to join in. Cost of entry: one value. Choose one value to discard. Place this value face down, on top of the other values you discarded.

v. After a really enjoyable evening you retire and have one of the best sleeps you have ever had. Rested and rejuvenated you speak to the Excursions Manager and find out that the first port of call has an incredible adventure that you would like to join. The price of this is not included in your cruise fare so in order to go on this port excursion you must surrender one more value. Place this value face down, on top of the other values you discarded.

vi. Repeat this until you have only one card still face up.

    vii. Last step in this exercise: enter your identified values in the chart below. Enter the one value that remained face up during the last part of this exercise in the first line. This is your most highly regarded value. Use as many lines as you have key values for (add more lines if your list exceeds 12). Enter the date, as that information will become useful at a later time.

Date:

1.	
2.	
3.	
4.	
5.	
6.	
7.	
8.	
9.	
10.	
11.	
12.	

Personal Values Worksheet

Congratulations! You've achieved clarity on your own values! Wow!

So what's next? Creating your own definition for your values and looking at how well you're currently living them in your everyday life.

Let's start with creating some definitions for your identified values. For each, you will provide supportive words that best describe it. You will use this worksheet in the next exercise as well.

Here's an example:

Rank	Value Name	Descriptive Words		
1	Integrity	Respect, truth, honour, telling the truth.		
2	Family	Togetherness, community.		
3	Success	Consciousness, integrity.		

Go ahead now and create your own descriptive words for the chart you'll find at the end of this section using the following steps:

1. Write each value in the column titled "Value Name," starting with your number-one value and working down through all the values you included in the last exercise.

2. Write words that describe your values. You can use the values list as reference if you like. You may find that some of the words you didn't use prompt you or are useful as descriptors for your chosen values.

Living Index Exercise

The next exercise involves gauging how well you're living each value, a practice that requires you to look at each value independently of the others and to identify how effectively you believe you're living it right now. Take care here: this is not how well you *would like to be* living each, nor is it *how you feel others* might see you living it. It's about how well *you* see yourself living it. Be as honest with yourself as you can.

Use a 1-10 scale, where 10 is high, and one is low.

Follow these steps:

1. On the top of column four, write "Current Living Index" (CLI). Using a 1-10 scale, evaluate *how well you are living that value now*. See the example below.

Rank	Value Name	Descriptive Words	Current Living Index	
1	Integrity	Respect, truth, honour, telling the truth.	7	
2	Family	Togetherness, community.	6	
3	Success	Consciousness, integrity.	4	

2. On the top of column five, write in Ideal Living Index (ILI). This is the level to which you desire to live the value. Your ideal may be the same as the ranking in column four. That's OK. It may be, as often is the case, a higher ranking. It's a very individual number. Be real about your ranking. It can be a stretch but must be achievable. See example below.

Rank	Value Name	Descriptive Words	Current Living Index	Ideal Living Index
1	Integrity	Respect, truth, honour, telling the truth.	7	10
2	Family	Togetherness, community.	6	9
3	Success	Consciousness, integrity.	4	8

My Personal Values Worksheet

Rank	Value Name	Descriptive Words	Current Living Index	Ideal Living Index

Reflection Questions

Now that you've found clarity on your values, let's look at the impact each has on your life and the way you choose to live it. This exercise allows you to focus in on achieving the *Ideal Living Index*. If you're currently unemployed, you can either skip questions four and five, or reflect back on a period of previous employment. Question six relates to leadership, including managerial/supervisory positions you've held and any leadership qualities you've demonstrated in your life (think self-leadership; leadership you've exhibited among family and friends; and leadership put to work in volunteer or educational situations).

1. What are you currently doing to honour your top values, and what can you do to better honour those values?

_____

_____

_____

_____

_____

_____

_____

_____

2. What would fully living each value do for you? How would your life be different?

_____

_____

_____

_____

_____

_____

_____

_____

3. If each value were to give you some advice, what would it be?

_____

_____

_____

_____

_____

_____

_____

_____

4. How aligned are your values to:

- Your coworkers' values?

- Your department's values?

- Your organization's values?

_____

_____

_____

_____

_____

_____

_____

5. Where (if any) are the disconnects? What actions do you need to take to rectify them?

_____

_____

_____

_____

_____

_____

_____

_____

6. Where are these values showing up in your leadership efforts? What is the impact and result to you, your team and your organization? Consider the impact on problem-solving, creativity, team-building, choice and potential for success in tasks.

_____

_____

_____

_____

_____

_____

_____

_____

_____

Creating Your Personal Values Statement

With your top values and living index action plan in hand, you're now ready to develop a Personal Values Statement (also called a Success Statement). This expression of your mission or purpose — based on work you completed in this and previous chapters — will prove a very useful document when you have to make personal decisions.

Your statement should begin with: "Success to me is ..." You may incorporate your top values in any way, either literally or through reference. For example, if freedom is a top value, your statement may read: "Success to me is cruising down the road of life, listening to sweet music." The statement is in pursuit of freedom, the fact that it doesn't directly use that word notwithstanding. This is a first draft; don't expect it to be perfect! Just start writing and see where the exercise takes you.

Once you've written your Personal Values Statement, reread it. Allow yourself to ascertain how closely it reflects the true you. Then leave it. Take another look at it tomorrow. When you do, edit and revise it as required. If you believe it's a true reflection of you, leave it alone. There's no such thing as "perfect" in this exercise; there's only "best" for you. That's what's important.

I have written Personal Values Statements for at least the last decade, and each one has taken a different amount of time to complete; the first took several days to do. After letting it sit for a day, I returned to it and was amazed that what I had written described me more closely than anything I'd written before. After returning to it a couple more times and making a few minor tweaks, I was still quite pleased. It described me perfectly! Just listen to your inner voice. You'll get to a point at which you'll know it should be left as is — at least for now.

These statements are to be continually updated. You may find that as you acquire the value, it diminishes in importance. For example, one of my clients, Julie, highly values solitude. She lived that value most of her life, but didn't know it because she never took the time to define it and make it part of herself. Once she did, however, she began changing things in her life so that solitude figured prominently in it. As that need was met, it fell out of her top values inventory, therefore affecting her Personal Values Statement.

Start by creating a first draft of your Personal Values Statement. At the end of this chapter, another blank page awaits your revised Personal Values Statement.

My Personal Values Statement version # _____

Date: _____

_____

_____

_____

_____

_____

_____

_____

_____

_____

_____

_____

_____

_____

_____

Using Your Personal Values in Decision-Making

Now that you have your values clarified and your Personal Values Statement written, let's put it all to use.

> *It's not hard to make decisions when you know what your values are.*
> — Roy Disney

Creating a Values Prism

First, an example: Sarah had worked in automotive sales for 20 years, but now wasn't sure if she wanted to continue in this line of work. Her children were off at university and she was searching for greater meaning in her work. Her days of feeling fulfilled in her job were over, and it was time for a change. Sarah had several choices, but was struggling to decide on one when she came to see me in a state of deflation. I had her do the values exercise, and she identified her top values as:

- flexibility

- fun

- independence

- variety

- contribution.

She knew she could continue in automobile sales. It was familiar and didn't take much effort. But all the time she'd spent looking at universities with her kids had highlighted the idea of going back to school. The notion had piqued her curiosity greatly. Bearing this in mind, I asked her to create a "values prism" that might help her with a potential next step in her career path.

This kind of prism can be utilized in a variety of life situations, and can shed light on such questions as:

- What should my next career step be?

- Should I accept a promotion at work or stay in my current role?

- Should I pursue part-time studies with my work?

- Is it best to stay in my current role or accept a transfer to another city?

- Which city is it best for me to live in?

The benefit of a values prism is the ability it gives us to look at each choice in a major decision and evaluate it according to how well it meets our values. By looking at each option through the value prism, decisions are made easier.

Creating your own Values Prism

Here's how you create a values prism (you can use the template on page 51):

1. List your values down the left column.

2. List your options across the top.

3. Rate each option based on how well it will help you incorporate these values in your life using the following scale:

   If the option fully meets your value: 3 points

   If the option only partially meets your value: 2 points

   If it marginally meets your value: 1 point

   If it doesn't meet your value at all: 0 points

4. Once you've completed the ratings, total them up for each option.

5. Analyze the results.

Let's take a look at Sarah's Value Prism:

Values	Automotive sales	Study psychology at university	Administrative work at a retreat centre	Part-time sales and part-time university study
Flexibility	1	2	3	1
Fun	3	2	3	1
Independence	2	3	2	2
Variety	2	2	1	2
Total	8	9	9	6

As you can see, Sarah had a tie between attending university and working in a retreat centre. To make a decision, she had to consider both the short- and long-term realization of these values.

In a situation like this, one value may attract a high rating *right now* but, three years into following the path, its merit may have diminished considerably. That is shown in this example. If Sarah chose working in the same industry, it may prove the easier route for now, but the boredom would likely set in again after a short time. Create awareness of what your real passion is and follow it. For Sarah, choosing to attend university may not be as rewarding as other options now, but it will be more in a few years when she is truly following her passion, and incorporating and honouring her values into her life.

Now it's your turn. Write a question below that you've been considering. It may be a choice of career, where you want to live or educational choices, just to name a few.

_____

_____

_____

_____

_____

Now try putting your values and options in the Values Prism.

Values							
Total							

Write your conclusions here.

Consider the following:

- What scored the highest?

- Was it the one you really wanted anyway?

- What are the next steps you need to take, now that you've made a decision?

_____

_____

_____

_____

_____

_____

_____

There is a blank copy of this template at the end of the chapter. You may copy that page as many times as you wish to use in decision-making.

Now that we've established your key driving values, have used them to guide us in the preparation of both a Personal Values Statement and a Values Prism, and have learned how to use it all for decision-making, let's assess your strengths. How can you use your strengths to bring about the goals you've outlined in your statement? They're one more piece in the building blocks of YOU!

Additional Personal Values Statement forms

As you revise your success statement, use this form. Duplicate it freely so that you have a fresh copy with which to update every year or so.

My success statement version # _____   Date: _____

_____

_____

_____

_____

_____

_____

_____

_____

_____

_____

_____

_____

_____

Values Prism

Values							Total

Action Chart

Action	Date	Dependencies/Risks

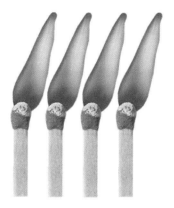

4   IDENTIFYING, LEVERAGING AND UTILIZING YOUR STRENGTHS

"What I know is that if you do work that you love, and the work fulfills you, the rest will come."
— **Oprah Winfrey**

In the last chapter, you identified your driving values. In this chapter, we will identify your strengths and help you get more mileage out of them. Leveraging your strengths allows you to apply them to their maximum potential and delivers an increased sense of satisfaction to your soul. A strength is a natural attribute, not a learned skill. It's innate, from within, part of our authentic selves. We each have our own sources of strength. None of us is good at *everything*, but we're each of us good at *something*. And as for those things at which we don't particularly excel, well, that doesn't mean they should be eliminated from our lives altogether. There's no reason we can't exercise every last of our faculties — given the right instruction, support and circumstances — even those in which we exhibit the least proficiency.

Because, as important as identifying those parts of your personality for which you have a particular strength is, spotting strengths that aren't your strongest — known in some circles as "weaknesses" — and developing strategies for minimizing their application is just as important.

A great way to identify strengths is to look at what you love to do. However, bear in mind that enjoying something is different from doing something well. When I was in my first year of university and looking for a part-time job, I got hired as a bookkeeper for a small business. I performed the job with proficiency, but really didn't like it. It always seemed to be an effort. I didn't realize it at the time, but I was using an area of *least strength* in this capacity: my numerical skills. On the other side of my strength ledger, find communication skills. I regularly speak in front of large audiences and totally feel in my groove when I do. Talking to others is one of my greatest strengths. I feel fulfilled when I'm doing it, and reassured that I'm in the right place, doing the right thing.

One of my clients, Mary, has struggled with a job she does well but doesn't enjoy. She drags herself into work every day, gets her tasks done and goes home tired. Throughout this chapter, we'll walk with Mary along her path as she identifies her strengths and works to surface from this less-than-satisfying situation.

Think of a time you felt like you weren't in your groove, when you felt unfulfilled and unsatisfied. You may have been performing your job well — perhaps so well that your boss kept asking you to do more of it — but, chances are, you were doing something that didn't honour your strengths. Note how that experience felt here:

_____

_____

_____

_____

Now contrast that with a time when you truly *were* in your groove, doing something that just came easily and produced good results. Chances are, you were drawing from an area of greater strength in this instance.

_____

_____

_____

_____

_____

_____

Once you become more aware of your strengths, you look at things differently and make decisions through a more magnified lens. You become more conscious of the activities in which you're participating, the choices you're making and the way you're perceiving things.

There are two things I know for sure about strengths:

- When you focus on your areas of greatest strength, you reach a place of maximum satisfaction and contribution.

- When you minimize your areas of least strength, you decrease feelings of stress and tension.

Think about a time when you weren't in your groove — how was your energy? Likely, none too strong. You may have even felt your sagging spirit in your body in the form of physical weakness or a heavy ache. These are the activities we want to minimize, fo-

> *"If human beings are perceived as potentials rather than problems, as possessing strengths instead of weaknesses, as unlimited rather than dull and unresponsive, then they thrive and grow to their capabilities."*
> — *Barbara Bush, wife of the 41st president of the United States*

cusing our energies, instead, on the spectrum's other end — the areas we feel great in. We want to harness these strengths and increase our reliance upon them in our jobs.

There are three perspectives on using strengths: individual, team and organizational.

Using Your Strengths from an Individual Perspective

This is about finding and using your strengths so that you feel good, satisfied and content. This scene comes by way of discovering what you enjoy doing and doing more of it. If you love details, the more you do detailed work, the happier you'll feel. It is to your benefit and will enhance your situation if you let your leadership and team members know of your fondness for the stuff. If your manager and team members know you love details, you'll likely get more detailed work to do. Contentment will ensue. Better still for your employer, your productivity will soar.

Using Your Strengths from a Team Perspective

Imagine if everyone on your work team similarly identified their greatest strengths and worked on optimizing them. You would have a really high-performing team with, ideally, every base expertly covered. Think about it: if numbers aren't your strength, they may well be a strength for another member of your team. If someone else on your team has creative strengths while yours reside in details, you could create amazing reports together. Detailed you could amass all the data, and your creative peer could take the information and transform it into a snazzy presentation.

More than once I've had clients tell me they hate doing presentations. "I'd rather have all my teeth pulled than have to stand up and put on a show. Leave me behind the scenes!" What would you tell these folks? How about, "Find someone else to do the presentation if it's that stressful." Obviously, that's a choice. Another might be to take a course in presentation skills in order to become more comfortable in front of an audience. We'll talk more about choices later on. In any event, on a group project with every member assigned to tasks that leverage his particular strengths, the job not only gets done with proficiency, but a sense of teamwork is fostered in the doing.

Using Your Strengths from an Organizational Perspective

A smart organization wants its members to use their strengths. Businesses naturally hone in on the bottom line, bent on increasing profitability and productivity. The fastest route to this destination? Focusing on individual employee strengths. Such an approach is not only good for the organization, but good for the individual. If your strengths are being exploited to their fullest, you're going to feel happier. Happier team members are absent from work less often and tend to stay with the same company longer. The costs associated with both absenteeism and the rehiring process are a drag on productivity.

So there you have it: three perspectives on strengths. Identifying and leveraging your own just makes sense.

Employee Engagement

"At work, I have the opportunity to do what I do best every day." Gallup asked more than 10 million people worldwide to comment on the accuracy of this statement in their own lives, as part of the research-based performance-management consulting company's employee engagement survey. Only one-third said they "strongly agree." In a more recent Gallup poll, among those who "disagreed" or "strongly disagreed" with this statement, *not a single person* was revealed to be emotionally engaged on the job. [v]

Studies also indicate that employees who *do* have the opportunity to focus on their strengths every day are *six times as likely to be engaged in their jobs* and *more than three times as likely to report having an excellent quality of life.*

My work takes me to organizations in Canada, the US and Europe, where I regularly bear witness to this phenomenon. No matter where I am, I discover people who fully use their strengths and are seen as great assets to their companies. They bring a positive energy to whatever they do, sincerely enjoy their efforts and perform their functions well. It's a win-win situation. What a perfect employment situation.

It's useful to point out that this balance extends beyond the workplace. It affects home, family, volunteer work, friendships and so on. The more satisfied we are, the greater the impact that sense of satisfaction will have on all facets of our life.

Identifying Your Strengths

Now that we've discussed leveraging strengths and how good it feels to be doing so (and how unpleasant the opposite feels), let's explore how to single out yours. There are four key steps:

1. Observe your strength level

In this step, you'll observe yourself and your responses to stimuli to identify some of your areas of greatest and least strength. Both are important to know as you move on to leveraging the former.

2. Get external feedback on your strengths

In this step, you'll survey the people who know you best.

3. Reflect on your strengths

In this step, you'll be prompted with questions to further mine your strengths.

4. Create your signature strengths list

This is the bring-it-all-together step, where you gather all your strength information into one place

Let's get started.

Step 1: Observation

This first step is focused on observing your own level of strength in a variety of situations.

In your notebook, title one section, "My Greatest Strengths" and another, "My Least Strengths." You may want to leave a few pages in between. Now it's time to engage in some self-observation. Each time you feel like your strength is being utilized while engaged in an activity, add it to your Greatest Strengths list. For example, I know that when I'm being creative, I feel my strengths are being used. More specifically, when I write, the time flies by. I feel relaxed and at ease. So I know that two of my greatest strengths are creativity and writing. Maybe for you, preparing PowerPoint slides infuses you with the same kind of energy. It may be the creative aspect of the task, or the sharing of knowledge it entails. Whatever. Take a moment now and bring to your awareness those instances when you felt a strength was being used. Use them to begin your list.

It's equally important in a learning exercise to identify moments that you feel drained, those occasions when you are being called upon to use your areas of least strength. Each time you feel spent while engaged in a particular activity, forced to use muscles that are simply not strong enough for the job, add it to your Least Strengths list. Perhaps the fact-finding requirement for putting a PowerPoint presentation together is tedious for you. If you procrastinate it endlessly, that's a good sign that it's one of your areas of least strength.

Your assignment is to observe your strengths — both your greatest and least — for the next week.

Step 2: External Feedback

No one knows us as well as we know ourselves, certainly, but there is value in getting external input on strengths. It can provide amazing insight. For this exercise, you'll contact five people you know well to ask them to weigh in on your strengths. Choose people who really know you — your boss, co-workers, family members or friends — from a variety of settings. Phone them or shoot them an e-mail. Give them a deadline of a couple of days. In addition to asking what they regard as your biggest strengths, ask how they see those strengths demonstrated.

As the feedback starts to pour in, add it to the chart as demonstrated below. Finally, thank the people who respond. They are taking time to give you an incredible gift.

Strength	How it's Demonstrated
Detail Orientation	You arrange meetings flawlessly, inviting the right people, finding a room when there often isn't one, keeping minutes and communicating to everyone involved

Strength	How it's Demonstrated

Step 3: Reflection

Now you have input from others in addition to your own observations regarding your strengths. In this step, you'll do some introspective work to mine for strengths, with prompting from the following four questions:

1. What activities give me energy?

_____

_____

_____

_____

_____

2. What am I doing when I feel most alive?

_____

_____

_____

_____

_____

3. What situations am I naturally drawn to?

_____

_____

_____

_____

_____

_____

4. What's easy for me to do?

_____

_____

_____

_____

_____

_____

Take time to answer. I suggest carrying this book or your personal notebook with you throughout the day to add to your responses.

Once you've completed the questions, review the answers. When you summarize the strengths you see there, you'll likely notice trends that reinforce your findings. And you may discover some new strengths. Whatever your list, it's absolutely right.

Now, as you did before, give a brief description of each strength identified via a combination of your own observations and others' comments. Add in anything else you feel is relevant to the exercise. Bring together your own list of strengths and areas of least strength. Add into the mix the observations of others.

Take your time with these steps and really consider if anything is missing. You will likely want to put this book down until you have completed this. Once you feel it's complete, it's time to create your signature strengths list.

Step 4: Signature Strengths List

In this step, you'll identify your top seven to 10 strengths. If you have more than 10, whittle the list by prioritizing its contents. For example, if you have 15 strengths, choose 10 that you would rank as ones and five that you would rank as twos. Then take all the strengths you ranked a one and consider them your signature strengths. These are uniquely yours. Even if you and a co-worker seem to share a strength, it will mean something different to each of you, based on your definition, how you use it, your experience with it and so on.

Next, make a note on how you or others observed that strength in action in the "how it's demonstrated" column. Let's take a look at Mary's Signature Strength list by way of example, and then fill in the balance with our own material.

Strength	How it's Demonstrated
Detail Orientation	Organize meetings Keep minutes Remember small details Don't let things fall through the cracks Pride myself in having the right information
Creativity	Great at PowerPoint presentations Find creative solutions to problems
Connectedness	Great at bringing people together Love strengthening the team Like to organize social events

Leveraging Your Strengths

Now that you have your Signature Strengths List in hand, focus on its component parts. Research continues to take us in the direction of positivity. Allow your signature strengths to be a filter through which you see the world. Let this document guide you in your work and life. Remind yourself of these strengths when going into meetings and taking on tasks. Keep the successes you've had using them — and how that felt — top of mind, and then boldly step into new situations that best draw on them. It's a good idea to keep your notebook handy and continue to add to the lists you've created. Strength identification is, after all, an ongoing proposition. But now that you've got a solid start with your signatures, you're in a position to explore how to best leverage the stuff. The effort is a valuable one. Leveraging your strengths provides benefits to everyone.

Accentuate the Positive

Leveraging your strengths begins with focusing on the positives, not the negatives. Hone in on all the things that you most enjoy and do well. As we've discussed already, the things we do well are usually leveraging a strength. But, again, be mindful here: there are exceptions to this rule. I have a friend who loves to sing, but can't hold a tune to save her life! I suspect she truly does know that crooning is not a strength of hers, but rather a pleasurable pastime. If you aren't sure into which category your high-performing "strengths" fall, ask someone close to you.

Increase the Frequency of Use of Your Signature Strengths

Now a little time for exploration. Think about the things you do in your life that most use your strengths, and also those tasks that least honour them. Ask yourself whether there's anything you can do to change the activities that require you to use lesser strengths. Is there a peer who possesses a strength in that area who might take on that task with greater ease? Is there something they're doing in the lesser-strength arena that you could take on more ably? Is it possible (and feasible) to switch tasks?

If not, and you find yourself really stuck, evaluate each task on a 1–10 scale based on how well your strengths are utilized for that task.

Communicate Your Signature Strengths to Your Manager

A smart way to leverage your signature strengths on the job is to communicate them to your manager. After all, you want your boss to know what you do well and enjoy doing. Besides, using your greatest strengths makes you look good *and* reflects positively on your manager. In turn, your contribution increases, because the more satisfied we are, the more productive we are. And on it goes.

This provides a great jumping-off point for a productive conversation with your manager. Prepare yourself for this talk. Your boss may not be familiar with the concept of leveraging strengths, so come prepared with some good information to share. Explain the benefit of doing so, and use some of the statistics presented here if you like.

Then share your signature strengths — those areas in which you excel and enjoy sincere satisfaction from your job with your manager. Tell him that your greatest contribution can be through the use of these strengths.

And while we're in the workplace, this may be a good time to review your job description. You may have an up-to-date version or one that hasn't been revised since you started in the post several years before. Either way, it's a good idea to look at this with a fresh eye bent on identifying those tasks and responsibilities that really honour your signature strengths. As you review them, take note of what gives you energy. Also notice what zaps your energy — both are good clues as to what you should focus on. When Mary undertook this exercise she definitely identified some tasks she didn't like doing. In fact, in describing one of them, she declared, "I just wish it would drop off a cliff!" This, she realized, was a task that destroys, rather than augments, her energy. Not good.

Build Your Strengths Network

Do you remember earlier we talked about the three perspectives on strengths? As we discussed the team perspective, we touched on the importance of knowing other people's strengths. Enter the concept of a "strengths network," populated with souls whose ready-to-be-leveraged strengths may not be yours.

Create awareness in your everyday communication and interaction of other people's strengths. Bearing in mind the home truth that, just because someone does something well doesn't mean it's a strength (it could be a well-practiced skill), start your observation. Be aware of the energy level others have when involved in a task. Consider on what occasions you see them having fun, truly enjoying a task. Those are likely strength areas. If you aren't sure, ask them! And don't be shy to share data points on your own areas of strength.

If your peers really aren't sure of their strengths, invite them to do the exercises in this book!

Create Awareness of Areas of Least Strength

Now that you have explored how to best leverage your strengths, let's look at creating awareness of your areas of *least* strength. Understanding what they are and deciding what to do with them is a key to success in utilizing your strengths.

It's important to understand this so you can decide what to do with it.

Have you ever had a performance appraisal in which you were told all the things you weren't doing well? Chances are, those are areas of lesser strength for you. The performance appraisal's comments thereon should serve as a red flag telling you to somehow shift what you're doing so you can utilize and showcase what you, in fact, do well.

You have three choices regarding what to do with your areas of least strength:

1. Get frustrated, irritated and unhappy. Some choose this path.

2. Give up and just try to do other things ... Or not!

3. Run from it! Any time you're asked to do something that isn't honouring your greatest strength, provide reasons why it isn't a good idea and make other suggestions.

We're applying a little humour here, but the truth is, you *do* have choices.

Here are the serious choices. If you are faced with tasks in your least-strength areas, you can:

1. Take on the task and do your best.

2. Know that not all tasks and projects will best utilize your signature strengths.

3. Find an expert in the area to mentor you.

4. Look for information on-line.

5. Use your network to fairly exchange tasks and projects with another person, such that you can leverage the best of *both* your strengths.

6. Ask for help.

Maximizing Your Strengths

Here are some great suggestions on leveraging those strengths about which you're confident:

1. Let your manager know about your areas of greatest strength.

2. Ask for assignments that leverage your strength areas.

3. Join task groups or project teams that need strengths in your area.

4. Build your strengths into your next performance discussion or appraisal.

5. Where possible, switch task with a co-worker so that both of you maximize your strength areas.

Minimizing Use of Your Least-Strength Areas

We can't all be superstars in all skill areas. Here are some suggestions for working with your areas of least strength:

1. If you know there's an area of least strength, work on minimizing the use of it. If it's essential to your work or life, look for ways to increase that skill. You may need to just come right out and say that *this* is not your area of strength.

2. Take on the task and do your best. Know that not all tasks and projects will best utilize your signature strengths.

3. Excel at what you are doing. Just keep looking for tasks and projects that do leverage your best strengths.

4. If you need more learning, search it out. Take a course or search it out on the Internet. There's an abundance of sources of information and opportunities for learning.

5. Find an expert in that area and invite them to mentor you in the skill.

6. Use your network to fairly exchange tasks and projects to leverage the best of both your strengths.

7. If it's something that's stressful, as it was for Mary doing a presentation, you may ask if someone could work with you to make the task or project really great. Remember: you can always ask for help.

Integration Assignment

Put your insights into action:

- Find opportunities to flex your strengths authentically.

- Take action on the items you listed for improvement!

- Create awareness of other people's strengths.

Action	Date	Dependencies/Risks

Now that you've identified your areas of strengths, how do you choose where to use them?

In the next chapter, we will delve into the deliciousness of life purpose. This is one of the most asked-about topics among my clients. Through the coaching process, as layers of history are peeled and clarity is gained, purpose begins to reveal its importance. So, what is *your* purpose?

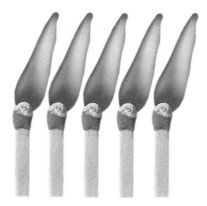

5   MINING FOR YOUR LIFE PURPOSE AND PASSION

"What I am living for and what I am dying for are the same thing."
— Margaret Atwood

Two of the questions I am most frequently asked as a coach is, "What is my purpose?" and "What contribution am I making?"

Your purpose is the job you were put on Earth to do and the impact you were meant to have while here. It's your conscious choice of the what, where and how of your positive contributions to your world. It's who you are and who you are becoming. It's not a vocation; it's your north star when you're drifting. It's an expression that defines your every moment.

The effort you put into understanding your purpose is exquisitely worthwhile for the articulation it applies to the subject of what impact you want to make through your

> *The great and glorious masterpiece of man is to know how to live to purpose.*
> *— Michel de Montaigne*

business or personal life. Defining your life purpose helps answer: *Who am I?* And *what am I here for?* It offers meaning to who we are in relation to the world around and beyond us. And meaning drives motivation. By understanding the *why* of our vision or goals — what we get when the dream comes true — we stay inspired through tough times in our pursuit of them.

Consider the successful people you know, or some famous individuals who clearly populated their daily lives with a sense of purpose. Think Anthony Robbins, Mother Teresa and Walt Disney. You will have achieved a similarly grand vision for purpose to theirs when you feel a sense that you're contributing, and that your gifts and talents are being used to their fullest.

For a number of years I did a lot of work for a client in Vancouver. The receptionist there was a woman who patently understood purpose. Every time I called, she answered the phone with a cheerful voice, pleasant tone and willing attitude. On one of my first visits to the office I asked her how she managed to be so positive all the time. She directed me to come around to where she was sitting and pointed to a mirror on the front of her desk. She told me that every time she answered the phone she looked in this mirror and smiled. That wowed me! In this way, she used her gifts and talents to impact every single person with whom she interacted, either on the phone or in person.

In this chapter, you'll complete a series of introspective and reflective exercises designed to mine your purpose. You'll explore your passions and engage the people who know you best in helping you to catalogue them. At the end of the exercise, you should be in possession of a deeper understanding of the unique purpose you bring to your time on the planet.

Passions

Where do you most feel alive, authentic and 'you'? Looking at these gives you insight into your passions. What could you talk about all day long? The more congruent you are with your passions the more fulfilled you will feel. Your sense of achievement will be greater.

In a class I was teaching several years ago we were exploring purpose and passion. One of the senior managers in the room was visibly struggling with identifying his passion. He had totally wrapped himself up in his work. His work had become his identify. Through a little coaching he allowed his true self to emerge. As he did this his face softened. A spark appeared. And then it happened: In the middle of a class exercise he stood up, closed his book and announced that he had found his passion. He explained that he had always been passionate about sailing. He had lived close to a lake as a child and had enjoyed many summers sailing with his family, and eventually on his own. His passion was clearly re-ignited!

Your passion may not be sailing. It may be volunteering at a hospital or helping at risk youth or making your own wine. It may be any of these or other things:

- Cooking

- Playing hockey

- Writing

- Rock climbing

- Music

- Photography

- Walking

- Dancing

- Reading

Every great dream begins with a dreamer. Always remember, you have within you the strength, the patience and the passion to reach for the stars to change the world.
— Harriet Tubman

- Surfing the Internet

- Playing the stock market

- Swimming

- Crafts

Having an understanding of what you are passionate about leads to an understanding of purpose. . Your passions, no doubt, extend across work, play, family and friends. If you're not convinced of the standouts for you, take stock of when you feel most alive. What do you enjoy doing?

Passions Exercise

The questions in this exercise will help you unearth your passions. Understanding passions is a key step in your path of self-understanding.

1. What are you passionate about?

_____

_____

_____

_____

_____

_____

2. What hobbies, events, situations or activities get you really excited?

_____

_____

_____

_____

_____

_____

3. In what activities and situations do you feel most 'in your groove', confident and authentic?

_____

_____

_____

_____

_____

4. What do you spend your money on?

_____

_____

_____

_____

_____

5. What activities would you feel a sense of loss about if they were not in your life?

_____

_____

_____

_____

_____

_____

6. How much time are you dedicating to your passions? (Most of us don't spend enough time on the activities that give us the most passion.)

_____

_____

_____

_____

_____

_____

Passions and Time

Often, we spend more of our precious time focused on areas that we are less passionate about or, to phrase it another way, we often don't invest our precious time in our areas of greatest passion. Let's see how you fare on this.

Complete the chart below, listing the passions you identify in this exercise. Estimate how much time (in hours or minutes) you spend on each passion in an average week. Ask yourself how much time you would *like* to spend on each (and enter that info in column three).

Passion	Current Time spent/week	Time would like to spend/week

Reflection Questions

1. Where are the biggest gaps between how you currently spend your time and how you would like to spend your time?

_____

_____

_____

_____

2. What changes do I need to make to better focus on the things I am most passionate about?

_____

_____

_____

_____

3. How will it feel to achieve these changes?

_____

_____

_____

_____

4. What hurdles can I anticipate encountering?

_____

_____

_____

_____

5. How will I overcome them?

_____

_____

_____

_____

Let's bring this together. Review the answers to the passions exercise as well as the time chart and reflection questions. If you are still unsure ask a few people that really know you for their view of your top passions.

List your passions below:

_____

_____

_____

_____

Purpose Exercise

Now that you've defined your passions, it's time to explore your purpose. In this section, we'll consider two views: an outside and an inside view. Identifying your purpose helps to answer the 'why am I here' question. Knowledge of this clarifies your path and provides direction. From this point you can align your thoughts, activities and associated results. What a powerful place to be!

An Outside View

In this first exercise, you'll connect with the people you know best. Although I truly believe we know ourselves better than anyone else possibly could, an outside view of this ever-so-important question can confirm or act as a laser focus on our driving purpose. And getting an outside view gives you an indication of what you're presenting to others.

As you begin this exercise, think about the people who know you very well, people with whom you enjoy a relationship characterized by trust and integrity. I suggest asking three to five friends, family members and co-workers. Once you've decided who to approach, the question to ask is simple: "What do you feel my purpose is?" Give them a timeframe in which to respond — a few days works well — and use the chart on the next page to record their comments.

My Purpose — Input From Others

Person Providing Input	His/Her Comments

Once you receive this input, look for common themes. What words or phrases show up more than once? Highlight them.

An Inside View

In this exercise, you'll be the one answering the questions. As with each of the introspective exercises, find a quiet place to work, take a few good, deep breaths and ground yourself. Don't go with your first knee-jerk answer — really work it through. Think down a few layers to what the deeper truth is for you as you address the following questions:

1. What's the difference you long to make?

_____

_____

_____

_____

2. What do you yearn to accomplish in the world?

_____

_____

_____

_____

3. Where do you feel you are fulfilling your purpose?

_____

_____

_____

_____

4. What's the legacy you want to leave with those who follow you?

_____

_____

_____

_____

5. Where are you most proud of making a difference?

_____

_____

_____

_____

6. Where have you experienced the deepest sense of meaning and purpose in your life?

_____

_____

_____

_____

7. What would give you the greatest sense of loss if you were not able to accomplish it in your lifetime?

_____

_____

_____

_____

8. If you had unlimited time, money and resources at your disposal, what's the problem you'd most like to address in the world, the one that would be most meaningful for you to solve (this could be something in your community or a worldwide goal). What level of satisfaction do you feel about being able to contribute in this way?

_____

_____

_____

_____

9. What impact would you have by solving that problem? How would achieving that impact make you feel?

_____

_____

_____

_____

If you are still unsure, look at it from a few other perspectives. Answering the following questions may give you more clarity:

- What do your responses in this exercise tell you about your purpose in life?

- What's the impact you would have by solving that problem?

- How would you feel if you had that impact on the world?

_____

_____

_____

_____

_____

The last step in identifying your purpose is creating a summary of the common themes and adding a description in for each. This is where you devise a personal definition of your purpose. In the first column, enter the common theme you identified in the previous exercises and then add a description based on your own comments and those of outsiders. Note that your description can include metaphors, such as the in the guiding example below:

Theme	Description
Teaching	Making a difference in others' lives, sharing knowledge and information
Family	Caring for others, needing to be connected to others
Comfort	Providing comfort to people who are in need, listening to them
Guiding	Acting as a beacon of light for those in need

Your Worksheet:

Theme	Description

Now that you've created clear definitions of your purpose, you're in a position to put them into a statement that articulates your unique place in the world. This expression of who you are represents you, your passions and your purpose. You can turn to it when you have decisions to make, are trying to understand why you reacted to something in a particular way, or simply to put a stake in the ground when interacting with people and handling situations. This personal expression of your purpose defines the impact you want to have in your life, and allows others to see what's important to you through your words and actions.

An example might look like this:

My purpose is to serve others through teaching, guiding and mentoring the people in my life, professionally and personally.

Try it yourself: My purpose is…. Oh, and I challenge you to dream BIG and choose BIG!

My purpose is:

Use this purpose statement to drive you activities, actions, behaviours and watch as your life becomes more in alignment.

You now have a handle on your values, strengths and unique life purpose. You're likely already making better decisions in your work and life based on this knowledge. In the next chapter, you'll create a personal and professional vision courtesy of various learned tools that can be applied across the board in your life, inside and outside work and family. Read on!

Action Chart

Action	Date	Dependencies/Risks

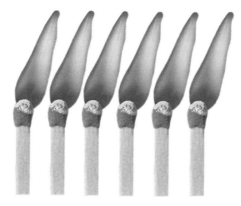

6   CREATING LIFE ALTERING VISION

"To the person who does not know where he wants to go there is no favourable wind."
— Seneca

With a solid foundation of where you are today now firmly beneath your feet, it's time to develop a vision for what's next. In this chapter, you will build on your values, needs, strengths and purpose to further your self journey. This is the transitional stage that will deliver you from the past to the present — before sending you on your well-prepped way to the future.

Vision is a term that's tossed around, without anyone ever attaching a clear or credible description of what the heck it is. Let's make that right. Everything you do starts with vision. Without it, you cannot fulfill a single, solitary goal. Vision is the awareness each of has of our unique needs and desires, an appreciation for which lends valuable clarity to what's important in our lives, and provides definition for our dreams so that we'll recognize them when they become a reality. Your vision can be for you as an individual, as an employee, or as a member of your team or entire organization.

Regardless, vision takes a snapshot of the future, and lays down the necessary steps for defining the path. This clear, detailed, sensory-specific picture of your tomorrow — that draws on your strengths and hinges on your values — is, ideally, so compelling that it drives you forward in its pursuit.

Visualization

World-class athletes regularly use visualization techniques to achieve success. Many Olympians, when interviewed after winning a gold medal, report that they "had the vision." They saw themselves winning the prize and drew from that crystal-clear vision with every action they took, every word they said, every thought they imagined. When British athlete Greg Rutherford scored gold in long jump in the 2012 Olympics — an event Great Britain hadn't won since 1964 — he credited his confidence and fierce conviction for his success. It was his destiny to win the gold medal he'd visualized for so many years, he told the BBC. And he was clear from the get-go: the gold was never go to be anything less than his.

In this way, vision is a precursor to success. *See* yourself being successful and then *actualize* it. Self-talk is hugely important in this process. I learned to water-ski on a lake in the Muskoka region of Ontario when I was a teenager. I remember, I watched others doing it and thought it looked pretty simple. "I can do it, too!" I told myself. So, with only a few instructions swimming around my brain, I eased into the cold lake water, strapped on the skis, grabbed the rope and gave the thumbs-up signal to the driver. I felt the boat motor roar and the slack of the rope shorten. Then: a firm tug and I was being pulled! I repeated the instructions in my mind and — voilà! — I was up! I looked around, letting my eyes take in the shoreline and the water below me. The moment of realization was profound: I'm water-skiing! My vision was complete.

But it was also short-lived, as it turned out. In the wake of my flash of satisfaction over my achievement came a flood of doubt. "I can't water-ski!" my brain screamed. And, with that self-defeating thought, I fell face-first into the lake! My desire had allowed me to ski; but my doubts had caused me to fall!

So it was that I learned that the process of creating vision must include a belief that what you are conceiving of is possible, even if it seems big. I have wondered often, since that long-ago summer day, if my belief in my ability to water-ski had been stronger, if I could have made it once around the lake!

Vision Story

A vision story is a description in story format of how you envision your most desired future. It takes a snapshot in time and describes the events it encompasses. It may be one, five or 10 years, or any defined time in the future. It is an expression of what you want to happen. Most of my clients have created their own vision stories. They provide the compass for moving solidly in the direction of their dreams. The path is there, you see: it's simply a matter of defining it for yourself.

A wonderful client of mine, Judy, wrote a vision story for herself that took place one year

"When you are inspired by some great purpose, some extraordinary project, all your thoughts break their bounds: Your mind transcends limitations, your consciousness expands in every direction, and you find yourself in a new, great and wonderful world. Dormant forces, faculties and talents become alive, and you discover yourself to be a greater person by far than you ever dreamed yourself to be."
— *Patanjali*

from the date of our session. Below is an excerpt of the work section:

"It is September 20xx and I am floating in my pool. The summer has been wonderful and now I enjoy the slightly cooler fall days. As I float, I reminisce about the last year. It has been a very good year. I achieved the promotion I had so wanted. I now have an office of my own with a bright sunny window that looks out to the green field between our building and the next. I have a very efficient assistant who helps me tremendously to complete the project my team has been tasked with. I now leave work at 4:45 to catch the 5:05 train so I can be home for 5:30. I now have dinner every night with Richard and Katie."

Bob, a 50-ish fanatical wanna-be golf pro wrote this in his vision story for three years from our session. At the time of writing this he was feeling stuck in his career, with only a longing for what might be possible:

"After many games on the challenging Pheasant Acres Golf Course, I have finally achieved par. The local golf pro was amazed at my prowess and recommended me for a role as part-time pro at Pheasant Acres. I have reduced my work hours in my full-time job and have picked up 16 hours as a golf pro. I feel I am doing something that has real meaning. I am helping people learn golf and it provides a wonderful source of stress relief. I am proud of my achievement. Rachel has supported my efforts and our marriage is now stronger as I have pursued my dream while still supporting my family alongside Rachel."

After writing this, Bob began taking steps to make this a reality. As a by-product of this, his work relationships improved and he was happier at home. He was pursuing his passion while still keeping his commitment to his family. It was a win-win for everyone.

Yet another client, a 24-year-old woman, Rebecca, wanted to meet a man and settle down. This is what she wrote about that:

"It's December 20xx and I'm celebrating my first Christmas with the man of my dreams. Over the past two years, I became crystal clear on what was important to me in a partner. With that information in hand, I courageously went on-line and entered my profile. After several dates, I refined my criteria and soon found my Prince Charming. And he is wonderful. He is kind and loving and generous. He loves me for who I am, and I love him for who he is. We have travelled together and he has met my parents. They adore him. How could they not! We are talking marriage and have set a date in the next six months."

I still remember Rebecca's eyes as she read this to me. She was alive, excited and ready to make this a reality!

The last excerpt I want to share is from Germaine. She had struggled with her weight since she was a teenager. More than anything, she wanted to lose weight and get healthy. And with a family history of heart disease and knee problems, Germaine was keen to get the weight off before her health was negatively impacted.

"It is January 20xx. I now weigh 140 pounds. I fit into the clothes that I previously put at the back of my closet. I feel good in my clothes. Walking up the stairs is a breeze, not a wheeze. I joined a weight-loss group a year ago and have consistently lost two pounds per week. I made it through the holidays and stayed on plan. That feels good. I actually started going to the gym that I had joined and never went to. I started with swimming twice a week and, after a month, added one night of yoga a week. And I called Cathy and started walking with her one night a week.

"I have started taking care of myself. I put the time aside for my exercise and meal planning. I schedule me time in my calendar and treat it as a meeting; a very important meeting.

"I am going to Florida in February and will feel amazing in a bathing suit.

"I did it. I was successful. I feel great and it was worth it. *I* am worth it!"

How is that for powerful! Can you hear the determination in this and all the vision story excerpts? The process is exciting and scary all at the

"A leader has the vision and conviction that a dream can be achieved. He inspires the power and energy to get it done."
— *Ralph Lauren*

same time (exciting because you know it's possible; scary because it may be).

Creating Your Own Vision Story

Now it's time for you to create your own vision story. Be clear and specific. Be bold. Imagine a vision so big that it's scary to say out loud. Let your heart open and your life unfold. Write the story so that it inspires you.

To get started, as with all the introspective exercises in this book, find a quiet place where you won't be interrupted for half an hour or so. Pack your writing journal, pen and the work you did on strengths, passion, values and purpose. Set your story at some point in the future (two years? five?) and write it in present *and* past tense. This way, you approach the exercise as if the vision has already happened or is happening now. That's meaningful.

When you're ready, take several good, deep breaths and allow yourself to get grounded. This is the place of inner knowing, the place where you connect with your true, authentic self and where your innermost dreams and desires reside. From this beginning, you create your most fulfilling future — one that leverages your unique stash of gifts and strengths.

Now set to writing for 30 minutes. To start, write the date you're working from (i.e., "It's January 20xx") on the top of the page, and give your mind permission to take you to that point in time. Put pen to paper, and begin. As you write, allow the expression of your most true self to flow, free of judgment or evaluation. The purpose of this exercise is to create, after all, not evaluate. Keep your passion, purpose, strengths and values top of mind as you work. And remember as you go: this doesn't have to be perfect or even complete; it will evolve.

Consider the following thought-starters to prompt you. No need to address each of these; they are simply reference points to spur your review of each part of your life.

Personal Life

- How you spend your time

- Community and contribution

- Hobbies

- What you enjoy most

- Your legacy

- What fulfillment looks like

- What personal success looks like

- How personal life adds to sustainability for you

- Which of your passions are part of your life

Family and Friends

- Who you spend time with

- Time spent with children and/or partner

- What you provide to others

- What you receive from the people you choose to spend time with

- What activities you engage in with family and friends

- Frequency and duration of activities

Home

- City you live in

- Style of your home (house, apartment, rental, ownership)

- Who is in the home with you

- Type of décor

- Size of dwelling

- Special spaces at home (hobby room, sewing room, home office, etc.)

- Electronics

- Type of vehicle you drive (if applicable)

Business

- Income

- Values and mission/purpose

- Business interests

- What you enjoy most

- How you make money

- Which of your passions and strengths are utilized

- Affiliations, associations and partners

- Geographic location of your work

- Travel time to your work

- Mode of transportation to your work

- Product or service with which you're involved

- Where you focus your time

- Number of work hours per day and week

- What your workspace looks like

- Who you are working with

- Awards you may receive

Health

- Level of health

- Sporting activities engaged in (walking, cycling, running, tennis, golf, etc.)

- Weight at that moment in time

- Food choices (e.g., choice to be gluten-free, to eat a greater balance of foods, to consume more fruits and vegetables, to go organic, etc.)

- Source of food (e.g., grow your own vegetables, buy local produce from markets, can your own sauces, etc.)

- Reducing, altering or eliminating medications (with your doctor's approval!)

To further assist you in the process of drafting your Vision Story, you might also ponder some general life questions. Consider:

- What's your life like?

- If your vision were as good as it could possibly get, what would that snapshot look like?

- How might your passions be expressed in your vision and work?

- What gives you the most energy in your life?

- What's the impact you want to have through your life and business?

- How is your business structured?

- How successful is your business and how do you measure success besides money?

- How is your business an expression of who you are?

- How does your business and full vision support your life purpose?

- How will you be different when you are living your vision? How will your relationship with yourself be different?

- How do you feel about yourself? What's most exciting for you as you imagine life from the perspective of your vision?

- What do your values add to your vision and how will you be honouring them in your life and work?

- What makes life most worth living for you?

- What will make your business and life sustainable?

- What do you need to create fulfillment in your life and business?

- How are you defining success — both personally and professionally — and how will you know if you achieve it?

When 30 minutes are up, stop writing. You should feel very proud of your accomplishment — you have taken a huge step toward creating your future! Now go ahead and reread what you wrote. Just read it through, without changing anything. If it seems really big, it's likely you've stumbled upon your true purpose, passions, strengths and vision in action!

Next, you can go ahead and edit your Vision Story. You can add more vibrant detail, clarify muddy bits and fill in anything that's missing. I caution you, however, not to cross off anything that seems too big. This impulse is likely only your gremlin showing up to stop you from progressing. Remember that the gremlin makes an appearance any time we show signs of positive change. Just acknowledge him, then put him away and go back to your Vision Story assignment with the knowledge that it actually *is* possible. As unlikely and unattainable as your presumed vision may seem for the moment, it's important for you to believe that, with dedication, support, hard work and unwavering belief, you can achieve it. Believe in yourself.

Now I suggest you put your Vision Story aside for a day or two before coming back to it for another pass. How does rereading it make you feel? Is it big enough? Does it best leverage your strengths, honour your passions and values, and provide you with the sense of contribution and satisfaction you desire? Make any necessary changes to make it so.

Reassessing

Now comes the time for you to start evaluating your actions and decisions, both at work and at home, in terms of their fit with your vision. Are you, in fact, living your vision? Are you making progress each and every day toward it? And are you honouring your passions, purpose, strengths and values in the process? You may want to schedule time every day to expand upon this vision you've devised. Often, I assign specific activities to clients on a weekly basis, each designed to advance their vision in some way. Use the action chart below and at the end of this chapter to create your own weekly activity assignments.

Making it Stick

With your Vision Story in hand, now's the time to commit to doing whatever's required, right now, to further honour your values and live your life with greater purpose, passion and values! List five things you will put in place *right now* to see your Vision Story through.

1. _____

2. _____

3. _____

4. _____

5. _____

Motivation is important to accomplishing your goals. Keep symbols around to remind you that you're moving along a path, and to re-pattern the inner landscape. Some of my clients:

- post pictures, goals or reminders on their fridge or bathroom mirror;

- hang up an article of clothing that they will soon fit into;

- display a miniature model of a car they want to purchase;

- put a symbol of an objective on the corner of their desk at work;

- send themselves notes of inspiration either by e-mail or post;

- cut out pictures of their objective and display them in a frame or somewhere prominent as a constant reminder;

- get an app to help with achieving their goal.

You can choose any of these motivational prompts or devise one of your own. Just keep your goal in the forefront of your mind.

The Beauty of the Vision Board

Wow! You've come a long way! You now have clarity on purpose, passion, vision and a personal Vision Story. Now it's time to take another step.

Whenever I lead retreats and workshops, a particular exercise is consistently one of my favou-

> *"Go confidently in the direction of your dreams! Live the life you've imagined."*
> — *Henry David Thoreau*

rite parts: the vision board. Through it, the vision comes alive and adopts a tangible form. And my clients love doing it, too, as it allows the integration of their vision and goals *and* the development of a visual representation thereof.

Many books have been written on creating vision boards, each presenting something a little different. The person engaging in the exercise should pick and choose what elements of it work for her. This tool is actually very flexible, and you can use it to create a visual representation of all or a part of your vision. I had one client who wanted a particular car so badly that his whole vision board was about the car. In the centre, he had a fairly large picture of the vehicle. Surrounding it, he had pictures of various automobile-related components: the engine, steering wheel, headlights, instrument panel and so on. He added in write-ups on the car and even cut out a picture of himself and placed it in front of one of the full pictures of his dream wagon. And, in case you're wondering, yes, he did eventually purchase the car!

Your Vision Board

Your turn! Follow these steps to create your own vision board:

1. Gather the necessary tools: namely, old magazines. Choose publications with a lot of pictures. Oprah's magazine is a great choice. Other good choices are sports magazines representing activities you enjoy, travel magazines, and decorating or home-improvement magazines. Scour your home and even ask friends for their glossy castoffs so you have lots to work with. You'll also need scissors, white glue and a large piece of Bristol board (though I find the thick, firm poster board easier to post on and it can be hung up or leaned against a wall once you're done). All of these tools are available at your local dollar or craft store.

2. Time to get started! Allocate two hours to the exercise, if you can. It's best done in one sitting, but can be broken up into two chunks if you can only scare up an hour at a time. Most of my clients tell me that once they get started, they don't want to stop! Find a place to work: a kitchen table or desk works well. Often, clients like to sit on the floor and surround themselves with their pictures. It's your choice, so long as you're comfortable and have allowed yourself a creative setting.

3. Review the Personal Values and the Personal Mission and vision statements you wrote. Your words will help inform your choices of what to include.

4. Search through your magazines for words and pictures that best represent your Vision Story. You may find an image or saying that resonates with you though you're not sure why — go with it. Cut it out and just let it percolate; the meaning may come to you with time. As you amass your materials, lay them loosely on your poster board.

5. Once you have a look that you like, lift each graphic and glue it into place.

6. Take a picture of your vision board.

If you're working with a partner on this exercise, spend some time describing and explaining what the images in your collage mean and how they collectively represent your personal values, passion, purpose and vision for your future. This helps to integrate the vision. Here are some examples of vision boards created by my clients:

So, I'll bet you're feeling a range of emotions now, from excited about your future to overwhelmed by the enormity of your potential. Rest assured that this is normal. Indeed, if your picture *didn't* scare the pants off you, I would tell you it wasn't big enough!

I suggest you post your vision board somewhere you'll see it often — maybe above your workspace or by your bed. You can make this your screensaver on your phone or computer, where it will serve as a constant reminder that every action you take in your workday needs to be supportive of your vision. Some of my clients who've posted their vision board at work tell me it becomes a conversation piece with their colleagues, who might even encourage the vision by reminding them of it. One told me that his co-worker, after seeing a theme of balance on her vision board, prompted her to go home at the end of the day! It's amazing where you can find support if you only let people know what you're working on.

In the next chapter, we'll put your creation into action through goal-setting. And we'll look at ways — some conventional, some less so — to set goals so that you achieve them quickly, painlessly and with a great deal of joy.

Action Chart

Action	Date	Dependencies/Risks

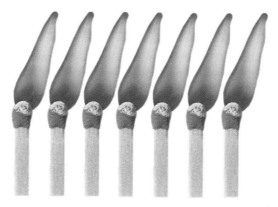

7   GOAL SETTING THAT WON'T QUIT

"Setting goals is the first step in turning the invisible into the visible."
— **Anthony Robbins**

Personal Goal-Setting

Now that you have identified your passion, purpose and key values, and have created a Vision Story and a vision board for yourself, it's time to put the lot of them into practice.

In a recent interview, Canadian comedian and actor Martin Short was asked to reflect on his personal and professional successes. He told the journalist that, for as long as he could remember, he has loved to entertain. He was actually very young when he started

> *"Goals are the fuel in the furnace of achievement."*
> — *Brian Tracy, Eat That Frog!*

defining his life's goals. He would be a comedian, he determined, and then set about seeing that through. In his mind's eye, he cultivated an image of himself as a successful comedian. He carried that image with him wherever he went. And he dedicated his life to making it into a reality.

Motivational speaker Tony Robbins, too, is celebrated for the clear vision he long ago created for himself of his personal, professional, spiritual and financial goals. A renowned storyteller, Robbins tells a great yarn of the humble beginnings that spurred his vision. He was at a very low point in his life when he decided to make a major change. He identified what was no longer acceptable to him, and drafted up the specifics of his new life. He described the wife he would marry, listing her personality traits, physical characteristics and so on. He described the house he would live in — a 10,000-square-foot castle-style home on the beach. He even outlined how his future office would look. In the time that's passed since that nadir, Robbins has gone on to achieve all of the goals he set out for himself. He was clear with his vision, and that did the trick.

Setting goals is, first, about having a vision. It's about knowing what you want out of life and then figuring out how to get it. Have you ever taken a car trip? Did you have a map with you on your journey to help get where you were going? If you didn't, well, how did you get there? Clearly, the absence of a map makes reaching a destination a hit-or-miss proposition. And the less familiar you are with where you're heading, the greater the need for direction.

A study tracking Yale University graduates found that three percent set goals upon their graduation. Twenty years after the event, that goal-setting segment of the alumni population were enjoying higher incomes than the entire 97% who didn't set goals!

Setting goals shifts you out of your comfort zone. Setting an objective that's a little more ambitious with each commitment keeps you alert, constantly reinvigorates your attitude and sets up your intentions for success.

There are five reasons why people don't set goals. They:

✓ are afraid of failure.

✓ don't realize the importance of goals.

✓ don't know how.

✓ are afraid of rejection.

✓ are afraid of success!

Each of these can feed the gremlin's hesitation and keep us from progressing. Be aware of any roadblocks on your path. Have belief in yourself that you can achieve your vision.

Goal-Setting Exercises

In the exercises to follow, you will set goals, starting big picture and working toward the more refined and precise.

The 100 Things Goal-Setting Exercise

Write a list of 100 things you would like to do before you die. Imagine all the different activities you want a part of in your lifetime. Think about what would make you feel good or fulfilled. Your list might include personal and professional achievements, places you would like to travel to, all the jobs you might like to do, the family structure you strive for, your volunteer ideals, and your physical, spiritual and financial goals. Eliminate all the mental barriers and focus only on those things on which your heart is freshly set. While there are certainly some impediments that need to be built into your plan (if you want to be a famous rock star but have a voice that makes animals run for cover you may want to adjust the dream from lead singer to drummer, for example), you should work hard not to let money, time, ability, experience or location be an obstacle. Be realistic about the barriers you uncover; in most cases, there's a way around them. Take the time you need to complete this. You'll probably find that you'll need more than one pass. How many times, after all, have you allowed your mind this kind of freedom to imagine a future? If you reach a dry point, I suggest coming back to it later and adding on as your mind dreams up more goals. Throughout the exercise, particularly during moments of discouragement, remember: Robbins talks of having written a list of what he wanted to accomplish in life when he barely had a dime in his pocket. The items on that list, once absurdly unlikely, have now become his very celebrated reality.

1.

2.

3.

4.

5.

6.

7.

8.

9.

10.

11.

12.

13.

14.

15.

16.

17.

18.

19.

20.

21.

22.

23.

24.

25.

26.

27.

28.

29.

30.

31.

32.

33.

34.

35.

36.

37.

38.

39.

40.

41.

42.

43.

44.

45.

46.

47.

48.

49.

50.

51.

52.

53.

54.

55.

56.

57.

58.

59.

60.

61.

62.

63.

64.

65.

66.

67.

68.

69.

70.

71.

72.

73.

74.

75.

76.

77.

78.

79.

80.

81.

82.

83.

84.

85.

86.

87.

88.

89.

90.

91.

92.

93.

94.

95.

96.

97.

98.

99.

100.

Questions to hone in on your goals:

1. List things that you're afraid to attempt. This question zeroes in on self-limiting beliefs. These are restrictions you've imposed on yourself about what you can and cannot do. But ask yourself this: are these obstacles *truly* prohibiting you from achieving your dreams? And if they are, how can you overcome them?

_____

_____

_____

_____

_____

2. If you had just six months to live, consider which of your top 100 you would you choose to do. Dig deep into your basic values for this. Are you doing those end-of-time things now? No? Then start. Make it count now!

_____

_____

_____

_____

_____

3. If you won a million dollars, what would you do with the money? This one asks you to take stock of your values. Money often limits our options. By eliminating this potential obstacle, you give yourself the freedom to attempt whatever you choose. If you set goals and work toward them, you'll be closer to realizing your dreams.

_____

_____

_____

_____

_____

Given that your list reflects your aspirations, goals and drive, consider how you felt putting it together. Did you smile? Did you hesitate on any, questioning whether you could do it? Be confident. Know who you are. This list opens a window to your future; don't allow it to close.

You have just made a good start toward achieving your goals. Your list is a reflection of your ultimate potential. If you set your goals, plan well and identify obstacles thoughtfully, you can make anything a reality.

Next, we'll look at the four components of life from a goal-setting perspective, and from there we'll look at setting goals in each area.

The Components of Life

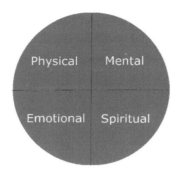

We're all complex, multifaceted beings. Every facet is important to consider when goal-setting, as each represents a part of one's true self, and should be considered separately. The four components are:

- Physical

- Mental

- Emotional

- Spiritual

Depending on the stage of life you've reached, you may have more to say in one area than another. Think of it like a pie chart; the pieces fit together snugly, each one closely related to the others.

There are three parts to you: your body, mind and spirit. Each part is one component of yourself, so we refer to them as your body-self, mind-self and spirit-self. Your body-self is part of your physical goals; your mind-self is part of your emotional, social and family goals; your spirit-self is part of your spiritual goals.

Let's take a look at each of life's four components.

Physical

Your physical goals are a function of how you take care of your body. They take care of it so that it can take care of you. My father passed away three days shy of his 95th birthday. He was always very thankful for all the care he had taken of his body over the years and partially attributed his longevity to that care. He was a phys-ed instructor in his youth and exercised throughout his life.

He played tennis almost till the end! He instilled a love of exercise in the whole family. When I was a teenager, we used to cross-country ski, toboggan, skate, swim and play tennis regularly. I learned early on that exercise doesn't need to be work — it can be fun. To this day, I still enjoy a variety of physical activities. Some common physical goals include:

- exercising regularly

- maintaining weight

- eating healthy food

- finding new ways to manage stress

- getting enough sleep

- drinking eight glasses of water a day.

Mental

What you feed your mind affects your whole outlook on life. Take time and learn — always. Learning doesn't stop when you finish school! You can continue the learning in everyday life — just seek it out! Think about what your life will be like in five or 10 years. You may travel to other countries, like England. It's a great place to visit because, among other things, it's rich in history. The Tower of London is one of the most interesting places in the world. You may have learned about King Henry VIII and his six wives. As you walk around the Tower buildings, you are led by a Beefeater (one of the Queen's guards). You mount the steps that some very significant characters from human history mounted centuries before you. It's quite an experience, but one you couldn't appreciate simply by reading about it in school. Life is filled with such wonderful experiences, in your own backyard and across the world.

You only need to open yourself up to learning — everyday — to access them. And that directive applies to both formal *and* non-formal education.

Learning opportunities are all around us. As an instructor, I learn from my "students" all the time. Did you know that despite all that we learn, we only use a maximum of five percent of our brains? Isn't that incredible? What a waste of good brain cells! It's quite humbling to think that even a life filled with ongoing learning will never even nearly reach its potential. Indeed, we'll never know *everything* there is to know about *anything*! Add on to this the rate of change in the information age and, when all is said and done, the reality persists: we know quite an insignificant amount of the information that is available to know. So just keep listening, learning, sharing knowledge and staying open. The knowledge is there, just waiting for you! Some areas in which you may want to expand your mind could include:

- Books on CD. Listen to something in transit to and from work. It's a great way to learn about something in which you have an interest. There's an abundance of CD-based leadership books available at your local library.

- Surf the Net. Learn about things outside of your daily scope.

- Read the newspaper. There are national, regional, community and special-interest papers. Each has a different focus and, sometimes, perspective.

- Spend time at a library or bookstore. Look at what other people are reading. Browse the shelves and pick up a book or magazine that you wouldn't normally choose. The experience helps to broaden your perspective.

- Find a new friend — someone of a different, age, background, interest area, occupation or culture from your own.

- Listen to music — any music. Pick something out of your ordinary scope of listening.

- Talk to a senior citizen. Admire their wisdom and add their learning to your repertoire.

- Write something — an article, journal entry, short story, poem or letter.

- Watch a television show that isn't in your normal stable of shows. Documentaries are excellent sources of good information in a condensed format. There are also wonderful travel shows that'll deliver you all across the world from the comfort of your own living room.

Spiritual

Your spirit is the part of you that you cannot see, touch or feel. It is what adds life to the physical shell you've been given. It's your desires, your capacity to care for others and all the other characteristics that make up "you." Goals in this area uplift us, nourish us and make us feel whole. Broadening your perspective is one way to feed your spirit.

Spirit is what's inside. It's not religion; however, to some people, religion is part of what's inside. Some religions believe that the spirit returns to Earth lifetime after lifetime, carrying with it the joys and sorrows of previous lives for reconciliation in this one. Hmmmm.... Whatever your religious beliefs (or lack thereof), you have a spirit within you. If part of your spirituality includes a higher power, include that in your goals. Your job is to make your spiritual self as joyful and peaceful as you can on your

"All our dreams can come true if we have the courage to pursue them."
— Walt Disney

journey. One way to feed your spirit is with goals. Some of those goals may include:

- Taking a walk in nature and listening to all the sounds; inhaling the various earthy smells; touching and feeling the leaves, bark and grass; really looking at how the petals in a flower fit together.

- Attending a religious service.

- Volunteering for something. Giving something to others without expecting anything in return is one of the best ways to feed your spirit.

- Meditating.

Emotional

Emotional goals encompass two areas: social and family. In order to keep your emotional side strong, you need to develop strong relationships with others — both friends and family. Doing so builds your support network so that when you need them, you'll have people around to provide guidance and support. More than that, in their time of need, you'll be there to help these people. Development in this area is about both giving *and* receiving. Remember that the universe will mirror what we create — if we're very giving to others, we'll get it back when we need it.

Emotional goals may include aspects such as:

➢ Strengthening family relationships

➢ Spending more time with children

➢ Developing new friendships

Goal-Setting Steps

Following these 15 steps will facilitate the creation and achievement of your goals and, ultimately, the fulfilment of your dreams.

1. Uncover the desire to set goals and plan.

How's that for simple? Any goals you set must be *your* goals, not anyone else's. You must have control over achieving the goals; if you don't, you're depending on someone else to do it. Not good. Make your goals yours!

2. Write your goals down.

By setting your goals to paper, they become tangible. This way, you can refer to them at any time to ensure you're working toward them. You can monitor your progress. Their hard-copy presence serves as a commitment to yourself.

3. Ensure that your goals are SMART (Specific, Measurable, Attainable, Relevant and Timely).

Specific: Goals must be clear and concise, so there's no ambiguity. Setting a goal of losing weight is not specific enough. A goal of losing 10 pounds by March 1, is more specific. The more precise you are about what you want, the easier it is to achieve.

Measurable: Quantify your goal. Use numbers that will assist you in clearly identifying a target. Ask yourself how you'll know if you've achieved the goal. In the case of weight loss, it's stating how many pounds you want to lose by what date. You may even put several measurable goals in the statement, each representing an increment of the total goal. Think: "Lose five pounds by February 1; lose 10 pounds by March 1."

Attainable: Do you have control over achieving your goal? If not, reconsider it. There's always the possibility of the unexpected cropping up and affecting your ability to reach a goal, but you have to ask yourself whether it's reasonable to assume you ever can pull it off. Do you have the necessary tools and resources to lose 10 pounds? It may be as simple as having a pair of running shoes for exercise and the ability and means to choose your own foods to assist in the weight loss.

Relevant: The goal must be relevant to you and your longer-term objectives. Once you've defined the direction in which you're heading, your shorter-term goals should support it.

Timely: Set a time frame for the achievement of your overall and interim goals. The longer the time frame associated with an ultimate goal, the more interim (or mini) goals you want to establish along the way. If your goal is to travel to Europe, it's probably a long-term goal. Setting up interim goals gives you that feeling of achievement in the meantime, not just in final completion of the goal. Interim goals may include the following:

- Save $50 a week, depositing it into a dedicated travel savings account.

- Read books on European cities.

- Speak to people who have travelled to Europe.

- Get maps to plan visits to a sequence of cities.

- Research tourist attractions, hotels, bus and rail routes, high-season timing, prices, languages spoken and currency.

4. Describe your goals in the present tense, where possible.

Use positive words and phrases. Leave out negativity.

5. Have faith in both yourself and in your ability to reach your goals.

Writing a statement of commitment is a good way to solidify your dedication to seeing your plans through. Your statement may look something like this:

"I promise to commit myself to achieving these goals. I will handle any challenges that may arise and create the success that I desire."

6. Do a force-field analysis.[3]

This exercise entails listing all the reasons you'll achieve your goal. These are the driving forces, the ones that really motivate you to achieve. Next, in another column, list the opposite — the restraining forces, or the reasons you might *not* meet your objective. In the losing-weight example, your force-field analysis might look like this:

Driving Forces →	←Gremlin Forces
• I will feel better	• I like food!
• I will live longer	• I have no time to make meals
• I will have more energy	• I eat on the run
• Clothes will fit better	• It's too expensive
• I won't wheeze going up stairs	• I don't know how to cook healthy foods
	• It's difficult to find food to eat at restaurants

7. Devise an action plan for overcoming your identified obstacles.

---

3. *Kurt Lewin; Field Theory in Social Science.*

In our example of losing weight, I listed six restraining forces that are potential obstacles. Let's take a look at how a couple of them can be overcome.

I like food! One's fondness for food doesn't have to be a barrier to losing weight. This initiative is about making small changes to when one eats, how much one eats and precisely what one eats. The plan needn't be overly complicated. By simply choosing one good substitution a day (instead of chips, choose low-sodium popcorn, say), you're making progress toward your goal. Eating while trying to shed pounds can still be a celebration.

I have no time to make meals: Plan out your entire week's worth of meals once a week. From that brainstorming session, do your grocery shopping. Save time by bundling meals together. If you make a double batch of baked chicken one night you'll have leftovers for chicken fajitas the next.

8. Create a plan of action.

List all the activities and tasks that must occur for goal completion, including a corresponding time frame. You may want to prioritize tasks if you have a lot of them. Make this an organic list that can change over time. Check off tasks as you complete them. At least 80 percent of wasted time is a result of people not being sure what they're supposed to be doing. Every minute of planning saves between five and six minutes in execution. That means 10 minutes of morning planning can save up to an hour of execution every day. More than that, you'll have greater clarity and will be bound to achieve your goals faster.

Part of the action plan for losing weight might look like this:

• Plan out meals once a week.

- Go for a walk three times a week.

- Write your goals on sticky notes and affix them to your bathroom mirror as a reminder of your goals and as a source of inspiration.

9. Visualize achieving your goal.

In the weight-loss example, visualize your body the size you would like to be. Don't just see your objective, but allow yourself to imagine how you'll *feel* when you're at your goal weight. The more vivid the visualization, the better. Conducting this exercise with committed passion can furnish you with precisely the incentive you need during those times when you're not feeling so positive.

10. Never, ever give up.

Keep your vision clear. Focus each activity on your eventual goal. Don't let go of it. One of the keys to success is to act as if you've already achieved your objective. Doing this puts you into an automatic mindset of success. Allow any negative thoughts to just wash away; invite the gremlin to step aside; stay on your path. With this view burning in your brain, your actions will follow and success will surely come!

11. Plan daily.

It's important to take your overall action plan and break it into daily planning. Every morning (or night, if that works better), review your goals and plans and identify the tasks that need to occur on that day Follow the 80-20 rule, where 80 percent of the value of what you do comes from 20 percent of what you do. In other words, if you choose your activities well, you'll use your time wisely and create the most favourable circumstances for actually achieving your goal. To that end, continuously ask yourself these two questions:

- What's the best use of my time right now?

- In five years, will this activity have been important?

Identify key tasks by prioritizing them. After writing down everything you need to do on that day, identify the order in which they should be done.

Visualize completing these goals. Be mindful of how you'll feel once you actually have. Now plant this feeling firmly within so you can draw on it anytime in the day.

Stephen Covey, author of *The Seven Habits of Highly Effective People* and *First Things First,* uses the four-quadrant matrix for prioritizing. The purpose of this model — which is said to have been introduced by President Eisenhower — is to identify the urgency and importance of all tasks to determine their priority in the overall action plan.

Four-Quadrant Matrix

	Urgent	Not Urgent
Important	1	2
Not Important	3	4

- Important, urgent tasks live in Quadrant 1 (top left). These are tasks that should be addressed and dealt with immediately. Putting them off usually has negative consequences.

- In Quadrant 2 (top right), the tasks are important, but not urgent. While not requiring immediate action, the tasks in this quadrant are still an important part of the planning process.

- In Quadrant 3 (bottom left), the tasks are urgent, but unimportant. These tasks — often the result of poor planning — should be minimized or eliminated altogether.

- In Quadrant 4 (bottom right), the tasks are neither important nor urgent. These are so-called backburner items that likely don't advance your objectives and are little more than time-wasters.

I love approaching this exercise with a clean sheet of Bristol board. I draw the four quadrants and add the labels. Then I assign each task to a sticky note, which I proceed to place in the quadrant for which is best suited. Given the hierarchy you've established, you'll likely tackle quadrant-one activities first. And if you realize one task here is too big, you might repeat the exercise, and break it into its own unique collection of tasks.

12. Set up rewards for yourself along the way.

These may include treating yourself to a night of pampering that includes a long bubble bath, playing a round of golf, some toenail painting, taking your motor bike out for a guilt-free Sunday afternoon ride, a facial or a night out at the flicks. Whatever the incentive, it has to be something *you* really want.

13. Review your goals often.

Doing so, especially when you feel really challenged and ready to give up, will remind you why you wrote them in the first place, and what you were feeling when you did. Allow yourself to revisit that place.

14. As you start to achieve your goals, give thanks to the universe.

None of this is achieved in isolation.

15. Have fun!

Setting goals for yourself is serious business, but making sure you have a good time along the way is paramount. Allow yourself the flexibility to be creative. This freedom lets you change your daily goals to respond to someone in need or to take advantage of an opportunity to enjoy life.

As you move through this process, you'll begin to have greater self-satisfaction, more inner peace and an enhanced positive outlook. There is nothing more empowering than taking ownership of your life. It's your life; create of it what you want!

Four-Quadrant Goal-Setting Exercise

Set goals in each of the four categories: physical, mental, emotional and spiritual.

Physical Goals

_____

_____

_____

_____

_____

_____

Mental Goals

_____

_____

_____

_____

_____

_____

Emotional Goals

_____

_____

_____

_____

_____

_____

Spiritual Goals

_____

_____

_____

_____

_____

_____

_____

1. Next, review the goals you've just devised and ask yourself a few questions about them.

   - Do you have control over each of them?

   - Are they SMART?

   - Have you used the present tense where possible in stating them?

   - Have you phrased your goals in positive terms?

   Next, seriously consider whether you believe you can achieve these goals. Having conviction in your plans is paramount to seeing them through. One of my clients, Tony, was passionate in his opinion that his goals would become a reality. His statement of commitment read like this:

   I will set time each and every day to take stock of my progress toward my goals. At the beginning of every week, I will review my goals and build their progression into the schedule for that week. I will celebrate my successes, even the small ones. I see these objectives as real, possible and achievable. Anything other than success is simply not an option.

Your turn: Write a statement of commitment for your goals.

_____

_____

_____

_____

_____

Force-Field Analysis

Often when we are initiating change, such as when we're setting or achieving goals, we're faced, head on, with obstacles, or reasons why a goal can't be met. It is helpful to anticipate these potential obstacles and plan for them. Being prepared allows us to manage these obstacles easily and effortlessly in the moment. We will always create greater success when we work toward a goal, as opposed to trying to move away from something. Have you ever tried to lose a few pounds, or quit smoking or take on a healthier lifestyle? Each are beneficial goals to our overall well-being, but there are challenges and temptations in abundance as we try to take on a new goal. When we are in alignment with the goal, such as losing weight, we focus on the benefits, and visualize succeeding with the goal. This continued positive focus creates more sustainable success. More about that later.

A force-field analysis allows us to identify these restraining forces which I refer to as "gremlin forces." This is important because, once we shed light on these gremlin forces, we can overcome them. The exercise allows us to thus strengthen our driving forces and minimize the gremlin forces, leading to ultimate success. Here's an example from one of my clients, Wendy. Her goal was to lose 25 pounds.

Wendy's Force-Field Analysis for Weight Loss

Driving Forces →	←Gremlin Forces
• Fit into my clothes	• Healthy food costs more
• Go to my high school reunion in 3 months feeling good	• No time to exercise
• Reduce high blood pressure medication	• Hard to plan out meals
• Not wheeze when I go up the stairs	• I like food!
• Extend my life	• Too tired at night to exercise
• Reduce load on my knees	• Dieting is not flexible

Wendy's focus was on her driving forces; all the reasons for her to lose the 25 pounds. She wasn't focused on the gremlin forces. With a focus on how difficult it would be, how much success do you think she would have? What energy would this bring to her objective? Clearly this would not set her up for success.

So armed with knowledge of potential problems Wendy mapped out her strategy. She set goals that allowed her to overcome the gremlin forces before they sabotaged her efforts. Her plan included the following:

- Set a budget for healthy food

- Every Saturday morning plan out meals for the week

- Shop twice a week so that she could adjust her meals creating the flexibility she needed

- Join the gym in her area and commit to going to the fitness classes 3 times a week

- Contact a friend that previously mentioned an interest in going for a walk in the evening and arrange to walk at least twice a week. (This made exercise more of a commitment and added a social element.)

- Put exercise as an appointment in her schedule and treat it with the same importance as any other appointment in her schedule.

Create your own Force-Field Analysis

Using the boxes on the next page, do a force-field analysis for those parts of your goal that you feel will be the most difficult to achieve. You may copy the blank chart if you need more than three.

In the lines below the force-field analysis, list your action item for overcoming any of the resisting forces. The bottom-line objective of this exercise is to consider how you can overcome any obstacles that may present themselves.

Driving Forces →	**←Gremlin Forces**
•	•
•	•
•	•
•	•
•	•
•	•

Visualize your success. Every day, at least once a day, re-read your goals and commitments. Allow the picture of achieving these goals to be crystal clear in your head. See it. *Believe it.*

Now that you understand both the driving and gremlin forces, look at how to minimize the impact of the gremlin forces and how to maximize the driving forces just as Wendy did in the weight loss example.

For each item you have listed, create your personal action plan on how to create success with your goal.

_____

_____

_____

_____

_____

_____

_____

Put your plan into your daily routine. Make it so much part of your life that your success is, simply, a foregone conclusion. Don't allow any other possibilities into your consciousness.

> *"Only those who dare to fail greatly can achieve greatly."*
> — Robert F. Kennedy

Persistence is Key

Never, ever give up. Inevitably, challenges will present themselves to you, and sometimes in abundance. Find your way over the hurdles and create success, one day at a time. Everyone en-counters obstacles — even the apparent superstars. It may sur-prise you to see examples of some of the most famous people's success rates. Here are just a few:

- ✓ Mark Cuban: Cuban, whom you may recognize from the TV show Shark Tank where he's an investor, started his first company, MicroSolutions, after being fired from a computer store. He licked his wounds and then applied his strengths to building a multibillion-dollar company. Oh, and he also happens to own the Dallas Mavericks basketball team, Landmark Theaters and Magnolia Pictures.

- ✓ Colonel Saunders: Harland Saunders trotted his now cele-brated recipe for fried chicken to 1,000 restaurants before he found someone who would pay five cents apiece for it. When he did, he grew his company to multimillion-dollar status. KFC is now a household name.

- ✓ Thomas Edison: Edison had 3,000 failures before finally scoring success with a little invention we now know as the light bulb.

- ✓ Jim Carrey: Carrey almost gave up after several films and a sitcom tanked. Broke and flagging, he persisted. Carrey soared on to superstar status, with starring roles in movies like *The Mask*, *Dumb and Dumber* and *Liar Liar*.

- ✓ Jerry Seinfeld: The first time Seinfeld walked on stage at a comedy club, he looked out at the audience, froze and was booed off. So confident was he in what he was doing, he returned to the same club the next night. His faith in himself was rewarded, this time, with thunder-ous applause. What happened next, as most of us know, is history.

✓ J. K. Rowling: Author of the Harry Potter series, Rowling was nearly penniless, severely depressed, divorced and trying to parent a child on her own while simultaneously attending school when she first set out to pen a novel. Her perseverance and determination vaulted her into prominence as one of the richest women in the world just five years later.

✓ Walt Disney: Fired by a newspaper editor because he "lacked imagination and had no good ideas," Disney ventured out on his own with little success. He filed for bankruptcy, but kept up the fight. Eventually, he built a vast and massively fruitful empire that encompasses theme parks, retail stores, movies and adventure vacations.

The Bigness of a Big-Picture Vision

A wonderful friend of mine, Bryan Bennett, introduced me to a powerful exercise in planning. He reminded me that a big-picture vision isn't accomplished in a day. It takes time, dedication and direction. And it takes a plan. To illustrate the process he had been using for years, he asked me to imagine a rose in full bloom. In my mind I summoned up an image of a beautiful pink bud, shining in the sun, fragrant and full. So real was my visualization, I could see and smell the flower. With a little direction, I could even feel the warmth of the sun of my face as I breathed in the rose's scent. Can you imagine it, too?

Next, he asked me to describe what I saw, which I did. "What do you think happened just before that flower was in full bloom?" he questioned. I said that it had been watered and exposed to bright sunshine to allow it to grow. "And what do you think happened before that?" he asked. I thought carefully about my answer before listing various things, including fertilization and trimming. He then reminded me that the rose had to grow from a seed into a small plant from which the flower would eventually bloom. "Ah," I thought. "Everything has a process." Very profound, Bryan. And so I took that process and applied it to the goal I was pointed at, and worked it backwards to the point of the seed of an idea.

My goal was to lose 10 pounds. At this point in my life, I was employed full time, had two small children and a new home. Such a goal seemed impossible. Every last doubt crept into my mind and I let the gremlin run rampant. How could I ever lose that weight? I didn't have the time to exercise or to cook healthy meals. My throat got tight; I could feel the knots in my stomach. The vision was too big, I told myself, growing ever more agitated over the unlikelihood of the enterprise. "Breathe, Anne," I told myself, and repeated this momentary mantra of relaxation. When I was ready, I thought of Bryan's directions and imagined my success a year hence. I broke the big journey into small steps which I now call The Success Rose. Working backwards, it looked like this:

20. Celebration of 10 pounds lost!

19. Buy a few new pieces of clothing for my newly svelte body.

18. 10 pounds lost.

17. Scour the magazines to find clothes that I think would look great on me.

16. Continue at the gym.

15. Find new recipes each week to keep interest up.

14. Go to fitness classes.

13. Put fitness classes in my schedule, the way I'd include a non-negotiable business meeting.

12. Find fitness classes that I enjoy.

11. Go to the gym three times a week before work.

10. Plan clothes to take to the gym so I'm ready for work.

9. Arrange with my husband to take the kids to daycare three mornings a week.

8. Cook two healthy meals at a time where possible so I can warm food up during the week.

7. Shop for groceries on Sunday for the week ahead.

6. Find healthy alternatives to eating junk food at night.

5. Post the meal schedule on the fridge so I can enlist my husband's help in preparing some meals.

4. Plan meals every Sunday.

3. Research gyms and choose one that's close to either work or home.

2. Find healthy recipes.

1. Create a vision board that represents the success of weight loss.

Your Success Rose

Now it's your turn. Create your own Success Rose by starting with the last thing that will happen prior to achieving your goal. Then ask, 'what happened just before that', and 'before that' and so on.

20.

19.

18.

17.

16.

15.

14.

13.

12.

11.

10.

9.

8.

7.

6.

5.

4.

3.

2.

1.

The Last Step

Now that your goals are written and ready, it's time to put your pursuit of them into action. Schedule time each and every day to work toward them. As you start to move toward your objectives, you'll experience greater self-satisfaction,

> *"The ability to concentrate and to use your time well is everything if you want to succeed in business — or almost anywhere else for that matter."*
> *— Lee Iacocca*

enhanced inner peace and a decidedly more positive outlook. There's nothing more empowering than taking ownership of your life. It's *your* life, after all. Make of it what you want!

In the last chapter, we'll explore the world of affirmations. This powerful technique makes implementing your goals easier, more effective and more enjoyable.

Action Chart

Action	Date	Dependencies/Risks

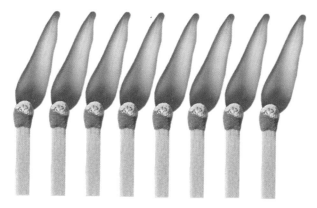

8   ACHIEVING YOUR VISION AND GOALS

"You become what you think about most of the time."
— **Brian Tracy**

This final chapter is about making your goals stick! We have already discovered that what we plug into our minds affects how we receive, perceive and react to situations. It has an impact on how we see ourselves and others, and how others see us. Our thoughts can either facilitate our infinite potential, or limit us to only what we have created up to today.

The reality is that whatever we choose to focus on will have an indelible influence on our daily existence. If we concentrate on our failures, we'll continue with that negative mindset and perpetuate a negative cast in our lives. But if we focus on the positive results we've enjoyed, we'll be much better set up to create further positives. Your belief system forms the basis for your outlook, and if you're keen to change the future, you must first change your beliefs. Among the most effective ways to do that is to adjust your

> *"Any idea, plan or purpose may be placed in the mind through repetition of thought."*
> — Napoleon Hill

inputs. Change the negative or even neutral messages you receive. Neutral messages are the hallmarks of a sitting-on-the-fence attitude, and don't generate any change. Negative messages just make you feel yucky. Change these messages to positive ones.

The Power of Affirmations

An affirmation is a positive statement someone makes about themselves and drives home via various repetitive methods. This approach to enforcing personal change can be very effective. There are key guidelines that can increase your success with affirmations. Let's explore them:

1. You must be the initiator of your affirmations — no one else can write affirmations for you. You must determine what words or statements will best address your issues right now. Still, there's an opportunity to make generalized statements penned by someone else your own, if they fit your requirements.

2. Affirmations must be repeated at least once every day for a period of three weeks.

3. Affirmations must be in present tense. Begin with statements such as:

   - "I am..."

   - "I do..."

   - "I look..."

- "I feel…"

- "I know…"

You might use "I will…" if you're referring to actions and attitudes that you'll employ today. For example: "I will choose an attitude of acceptance when faced with challenging situations."

4. Use only positive words. If your affirmation is centred on weight loss, an affirmation of "I will focus on not eating as much" will actually direct your subconscious to focus *more* on food. If you change that declaration to "I will focus on eating foods that are healthy, nutritious and taste good," you'll likely achieve greater success. The trick is to behave as if you've already achieved your affirmation.

5. Remember the principle of attraction: namely, that we attract the people and events we desire. If you believe you're opinionated, say, you'll serve as a magnet to other people with this trait. But if you alter your belief system to one that is open to ideas, you'll begin to attract people who are similarly open.

6. If you've been bombarding your subconscious for many years with negative thoughts, it is critical that you employ your positive affirmations repeatedly throughout your day.

7. Listen to your body and mind. Notice the subtle changes in how you feel and behave, and in how you initiate actions. These things are clues to how you're doing with your affirmation.

8. Change or modify your affirmations as you feel is necessary to most accurately reflect what you need in the moment.

9. Energy is added to your current affirmations by giving thanks for the affirmations that have been working for you. Remember the higher power that is at work.

10. Remind yourself that the only thing stopping you from creating what you want in the world is your own beliefs.

Affirmation Types

There are five unique types of affirmation statements. They are: your own affirmation statements, daily positive statements, rhyming affirmations, poem affirmations and "something wonderful" statements.

Let's take a look at each.

1. Your Own Affirmation Statements

Read the following statements, putting check marks beside any statements that resonate with you as you put together your own affirmations.

➢ I believe in me.

➢ I am unique and special.

➢ I am number one, numero uno.

➢ The most important relationship I have is with me.

➢ I choose the frame from which I see the world — I can be really happy with what is, or really unhappy with what isn't.

➢ When I need strength it will come.

- ➤ I am strong and capable.

- ➤ I have faith that I will be guided on my journey.

- ➤ I will never please everyone — and that's OK.

- ➤ I will break free from the chains that hold me down so that I can create.

- ➤ I am a good person.

- ➤ I take one step at a time.

- ➤ I express myself.

- ➤ The expectations I have of myself are real and attainable.

- ➤ I follow what's in my heart.

- ➤ I will make each day count.

- ➤ All the wonders I seek are within me.

- ➤ I am peaceful in moments of stress.

- ➤ I have the strength within to conquer the challenges put before me.

- ➤ I will take care of me today.

- ➤ My strength comes from within and from my connection with higher powers.

- ➤ I feel peaceful and serene.

- ➤ I am a good person.

- ➤ I like myself just as I am.

- ➤ I choose to respond positively to people.

- ➤ I choose not to be critical.

- ➤ I love my life.

- ➤ I choose peace where there has not been any.

- ➤ I will add in all the elements of my life as necessary.

- ➤ I have the will to live.

- ➤ I will live, love and laugh.

- ➤ I see the world through God's eyes.

- ➤ I love and accept others.

- ➤ I nurture my spirituality.

- ➤ I love my soul.

- ➤ I will be who I choose to be.

- ➤ I will be guided to the light of self-discovery.

- ➤ I feel good about myself and my world.

- ➤ I accept who I am.

- ➤ I accept the things I cannot change.

- ➤ I freely am who I am.

- ➢ I will live life with vigour and love.

- ➢ I express myself freely.

- ➢ I love living.

- ➢ I am free to see life as it is.

- ➢ I seek out people who affirm *my* ideals, not those of society or the media.

- ➢ I can do it.

- ➢ I am my own person.

- ➢ I define who I am.

- ➢ I am a wonderful person.

- ➢ I like my body.

- ➢ I am free to make decisions.

- ➢ I am responsible for my life.

- ➢ I am accountable for my actions.

- ➢ I choose to view my life positively.

- ➢ I will replace my old, damaging self-messages with new, healthy ones.

- ➢ I will take the time to see the beauty and wonder of life.

- ➢ I will inhale life with every breath.

- ➢ I choose to make today a good day.

- ➢ I choose to leave my limitations behind.

- ➢ I forgive myself and others so that I may move on.

- ➢ I will give the most of myself today.

- ➢ I will choose how I use my time.

- ➢ I can do anything I put my mind to.

- ➢ I will focus on activities that get me closer to my goal.

- ➢ I am the only one who can make me feel guilty.

- ➢ I am free to be all I choose to be.

- ➢ I am my best when I choose to be myself.

- ➢ I am a product of my thoughts.

- ➢ I will live in the moment.

- ➢ I will trust my instincts.

- ➢ I have the energy, attitude and will to accomplish anything I choose.

- ➢ I will overcome frustration with courage.

- ➢ I surround myself with people who like me for who I am.

- ➢ I am brave: I will survive.

- ➢ I will focus my energy on the positive things in my life.

- ➢ I embrace change.

- ➢ I have faith that everything happens for a reason.

- ➢ I have faith that I will be guided to what's right for me.

- ➢ I have faith in myself that I can conquer all that is put in my path.

- ➢ My future will take me to wonderful new places.

- ➢ I will find the opportunity to learn in all challenges.

- ➢ People will still love me regardless of how I look. I accept me, and that's the only thing that counts.

- ➢ I will be compassionate and good to myself today.

- ➢ Perfectionism won't create an unworkable position; it won't stop me from creating what I want.

- ➢ I will share my learning with others.

- ➢ I will proceed with my life, one step at a time.

- ➢ I am glad to be me.

- ➢ I will savour every moment, adding each to the cornucopia we call life.

- ➢ I will actively seek out positive energy sources for my life.

- ➢ I value and respect myself.

- ➢ I am a wonderful human being.

➢ I am a beautiful human being.

➢ I won't feel guilty for taking care of myself.

➢ I will persist until I am triumphant.

➢ I will dream great dreams and make them come true.

➢ I choose an attitude of success.

➢ I believe in myself.

➢ Yes, I can!

➢ If at first I don't succeed, I will try another approach.

➢ For every obstacle there is a solution.

➢ Whatever my mind can conceive of and believe in, I can achieve.

As you look back at the statements you put a check mark next to, choose a few that most resonate with you. Put a second check mark next to those. Allow these to be some of your affirmations.

2. Daily Positive Statements

Once each day, choose one of the following daily statements and repeat it to yourself. Choose a different positive statement each week.

- Today, once again, the heavens pour golden light upon me. This light caresses my thoughts, soothes my mind and washes away my worries. Today, I have my gift, to share or to squander. I will make today count.

- The success I am reaching for is attainable. My efforts will produce the results I imagine: they will lead me in the direction I desire: my destiny, the reason I am here on this planet at this point in time. I will feel the joy, be the joy and share the joy.

- Today begins a new week, a new opportunity to create great things. My seconds turn into minutes, into hours, into days, into weeks. I will choose carefully how I use this precious time. I will think a success, see a success and be a success.

- Today is a day of energy. Today, I will look at how to increase my personal energy and vitality. I will change habits that will affect today, and make the rest of my life more fulfilling. It's all in my hands. I will make a difference. I will make a change.

- I will not let the day fool me: It's a very lucky day. Today, I will make a great contribution to life. I will savour it!

- Today is a day of choice. I will be presented with options, some of which will challenge me to deviate from my chosen direction. Today, I will triumph, will make my own sun shine high in the sky, will allow the clouds of doubt and anxiety to blow away. I will make today count: I only have one chance to live this day.

- Today is a day of silence. I am given this gift to allow choice and freedom of words. I will allow them to flow into my life today. I will focus on my goal today.

- We will always be confronted with obstacles. Many of these are sent to challenge me, to test my will and determination. I make decisions every day on how I will overcome and conquer these impediments. I will make today count. I will leap higher over these obstacles than I ever have. I will rejoice in my triumphs!

- Today is a day of wonder. "I wonder what my life will be like in 10 years." "I wonder what I will do when I retire." "I wonder what I've done with my life." Today, I will allow myself the gift of reflection and introspection. I will look at my life and where I've been. I will chart where I want to be. I will follow my dreams, follow my heart. I will be the person I want to be and create what I desire in my life.

- Today, I am given the gift of light. I may shine my light wherever I desire. I may shine it on my gift to advance my steps or on those around me who are in need of it. Today is a choice. Make it worth it!

- Today, I am given the gift of peace. I will allow the peace to permeate my body. I will invite it to fill every nook and cranny. I will see it, feel it, experience it and then allow myself the gift of sharing it with others. It's a choice.

- Today is a momentous day. Change has begun! The world as I know it will never be the same. I have opened a door that cannot be closed without brute force — a strength of negative proportions that I don't want to have. I will channel my energy in the positive flow I've begun. I will see my success.

- Question of the day: Am I going to be a success in my journey, or will I be someone who always wished they had been a success? There's really only one limitation: me. I will make positive choices today.

- Today, I will be given the gift of ideas. Today, my mind will work hard on developing the notions that have been rattling around inside it. I will write a book in my mind about my path. Today is a day of greatness.

- Today is the day that I transfer all those great ideas and thoughts to paper. Today, I begin to influence others. I will allow my energy to flow freely. Today, I will permit the blocks of procrastination and self-doubt to wash away and make way for my greatness.

- Progress is always a continuous journey, with hills and valleys along the way. My goal is to learn to navigate through the course in a balanced, positive way. There really is no obstacle too great for a person with a vision and purpose. Today is a day of great change, and today I will navigate successfully, and at the end of the day I will have progressed along my path. I will choose what steps I will take, for each moment I am blessed with today, and progress will be made.

- Today I will have the strength to overcome the obstacles in my life.

- Today, I'll choose what path I'll follow. I'll choose my destiny and success. I'll choose who I'll affect and what my own potential is. It's my choice.

- Today is my day to make of it what I want. It's an empty canvas on which I can paint whatever I choose. It's up to me.

- Today, I will imagine I am planting a seed that will grow and develop into a beautiful flower. The seed needs to be nurtured and cared for, and then it will bloom. I am the seed. I will take care of me so that I may grow and develop into that lovely blossom.

- I will accept today's challenges and learn from them.

3. Rhyming Affirmations

Diana Cooper, author of *A Time for Transformation: How to Awaken to Your Soul's Purpose and Claim Your Power*, suggests that rhyming affirmations are stronger than the rest. Affirmations must pass through mental sensors — the gremlin — that decide where they fit in our belief sets. Gremlins will reject them if they don't fit anywhere; Cooper says rhythm and rhyme counter that process. They serve to lull that internal sensor and allow the affirmations entry to the subconscious. This way, the belief system is changed, and the benefits enjoyed, sooner. An example of this is illustrated in this affirmation of self-worth:

> *Today I choose to be me,*
> *I choose to be free.*
> *To feel good inside,*
> *I'm no longer along for the ride.*
> *I'm in the driver's seat,*
> *And now I feel complete.*
> *I now choose to believe in me,*
> *For all to see.*
> *The new me,*
> *As I choose to be.*
> **— Anne Rose**

Write a rhyming affirmation for yourself, describing your transformation.

_____

_____

_____

_____

_____

_____

_____

_____

4. Poem affirmations

Choose a poem that represents your view on life, and start each day by reciting it. It will set the tone for the day. Here's an example:

We sow our thoughts,
And we reap our actions.
We sow our actions,
And we reap our habits.
We sow our habits,
And we reap our character.
We sow our character,
And we reap our destiny.
— Anonymous

5. "Something Wonderful" statements

Several years ago, I attended a motivational talk by Zig Ziglar. There, he shared his thoughts on how to more positively view the world. When I left, I felt optimistic and energized. I was ready to take on the world. One of his key recommended techniques was to start every morning by telling yourself, "Something wonderful will happen to me today." He challenged us to do this for two weeks. It sounded like a good idea when I was sitting in an auditorium of 500 people, all of whom were buying into it, but when I awoke the next morning and remembered my promise, I felt considerably less positive. Still, I got up, went to the mirror, looked myself in the face and said, "Something wonderful will happen to me today." It didn't feel very natural, but I pursued. Each morning for two weeks I did this. And each morning it got easier and more natural. Soon, I would hear the *Hallelujah* chorus in my head when something wonderful *did* happen. It made me aware of all the wonderful things that were happening in my life. It was good. Very good.

Your turn: In the space below write the affirmations that support your vision, purpose, passion and strengths. Go back through all five types of affirmations and create your own affirmations.

My Affirmations

_____

_____

_____

_____

_____

_____

_____

_____

_____

Action Chart

Action	Date	Dependencies/Risks

ANNE'S STORY

Having journeyed together, the time is right for me to share some of my personal details with you. So here is my story: Over 20 years ago, I began searching for true meaning in my life. Through various courses and research, I eventually became a career leadership and communications trainer. In the period since, I've served on the faculty of training organizations and educational institutions, travelled to some amazing parts of the world, experienced diverse cultures and been introduced to many new perspectives on life. On a daily basis, a big part of my learning derives from two amazing sons who challenge me in ways others can't. I am incredibly fortunate to have strong relationships with both boys. My role as mum has always come first, but I've been challenged by the demands of work and the demands of life. This has provided wonderful learning along my journey.

Professionally over this two-decade period, I have been a senior-level director at a large telecommunications company, achieved seven designations in the coaching and learning arena, and built a successful coaching and training company. All of this has enabled me to create workshops in the material I've included in this book. Every workshop I do brings about incredible transformations in my clients. Emotional baggage gets left behind in the room and participants leave lighter, more focused, and abundantly more clear about themselves and their future. Relationships get stronger and more defined. Boundaries get put in place and comfortably monitored. Life improves. What a joy it is to witness these positive personal makeovers! And what a pleasure it is to have helped facilitate them.

Now Anne delivers keynote sessions, coaches and delivers training sessions to guide people on the path to igniting their purpose, passion, vision and strengths.

For more learning tools and information on how to reach Anne, to find out where she is appearing or to book her, visit www.innergizedsolutions.com.

---

i http://dictionary.reference.com/browse/power

ii http://www.merriam-webster.com/dictionary/self-actualize

iii http://sivers.org/maslow

iv http://dictionary.reference.com/browse/value

v http://www.gallup.com/consulting/61/Strengths-Development.aspx

BIBLIOGRAPHY